PHENOMENOLOGY AND INTERSUBJECTIVITY

PHENOMENOLOGY AND INTERSUBJECTIVITY

CONTEMPORARY INTERPRETATIONS OF THE INTERPERSONAL SITUATION

by

THOMAS J. OWENS
Boston College

MARTINUS NIJHOFF / THE HAGUE / 1970

ISBN 90 247 5023 7

PRINTED IN THE NETHERLANDS

She

to whom this book is dedicated

will know it when she sees it

TABLE OF CONTENTS

INTRODUCTION

Dialogue and communication have today become central concepts in contemporary man's effort to analyze and comprehend the major roots of conflict that threaten our twentieth-century world. Underlying all attempts at dialogue, however, is the presupposition that it is ontologically possible for men to reach one another and to communicate meaningfully. It is to this most basic question – of the possibility and the limits of interpersonal relationships – that various phenomenologies of intersubjectivity direct themselves.

Both the topic (intersubjectivity) and the method (phenomenology) are relative newcomers to philosophy and in a sense they arrived together. Ever since Descartes, philosophers have labored to explain how a subject knows an *object*. But not until the twentieth century did they begin to ask the much more fundamental and vastly more mysterious question – how does one subject encounter another subject precisely *as another subject*?

The problem of intersubjectivity is thus one that belongs in a quite special way to contemporary philosophy. "Classical philosophy used to leave it strangely alone," says Emmanuel Mounier. "If you ennumerate the major problems dealt with by classical philosophy, you have knowledge, the outside world, myself, the soul and the body, the mind, God, and the future life – the problem created by association with other people never assumes in classical philosophy the same importance as the other problems."[1]

Phenomenology, too, is a newcomer to the philosophical scene, especially in America. European professors fleeing the Nazi terror brought it here but many years went by before it gained recognition and status as a legitimate method of philosophical inquiry. In more recent years it has received wider propagation and greater acceptance. European source material is becoming more available through translations of continental phenomenologists. Gen-

[1] Emmanuel Mounier, *Existentialist Philosophies,* (trans. Eric Blow), New York, Macmillan, 1949, p. 72.

uinely original phenomenological works by American philosophers are beginning to appear. And though phenomenology is still far from being a truly major philosophical force in this country, its future here, in the eyes of some observers, looks bright. Thus, Profesor James M. Edie recently introduced a selection of original American studies in phenomenology with the observation that, in the years to come, the decade of the 1960's would be seen in retrospect as "the period when the phenomenological movement finally took root in our philosophical soil and became an active and creative force in its own right."[2]

One of the most tantalizing problems raised by European phenomenologists from the earliest days of the movement has been the problem of intersubjectivity. And one would think that it can hardly become less central an issue as phenomenology develops in the United States. For in today's turbulent America many of our greatest crises are social ones, and with the even closer interpersonal contacts that must follow as seventy-five per cent of our population concentrates in urban centers, not only social scientists but philosophers, too, will be forced to focus increasingly on the whole area of intersubjectivity. The American philosophical experience, of course, has always had its own unique characteristics and there is thus reason to think that any phenomenology of intersubjectivity developed here will exhibit distinctive features of its own. But in the development of such a native theory, familiarity and acquaintance with European efforts will undoubtedly prove useful and helpful.

This book does not aim at a comprehensive survey of the various studies of intersubjectivity made by European scholars. Rather it has a much more modest goal – to present simply a sampling of that research by examining the views of three phenomenologists (two are German, one is French) who have worked on the problem of intersubjectivity. The three views presented here differ widely from one another in their approach, content and conclusions. This diversity stems from the fact that there is no unanimity either about the general parameters of the question of intersubjectivity or about exactly what phenomenology is as a philosophical discipline. This twofold lack of unanimity admittedly complicates discussion of the issue but it can

[2] James M. Edie, ed., *Phenomenology in America,* Chicago, Quadrangle, 1967, p. 7. Two university presses, at Northwestern and at Duquesne, publish a distinguished collection of works in phenomenology, both translations and original studies. The growing interest in phenomenology in the United States is evidenced in the increasing number of books on the subject that are put out by commercial publishers and intended for the undergraduate market. One such recent volume is the excellent anthology published in paperback, *Phenomenology: The Philosophy of Edmund Husserl and Its Interpretation,* ed. Joseph J. Kockelmans, New York, Doubleday, 1967.

also be seen as carrying certain advantages. Thus, the lack of agreement about the exact limits of the question means that the problem of intersubjectivity has been studied from multiple perspectives by philosophers with different interests and different concerns. And the parallel disagreement about the meaning of phenomenology has undoubtedly made the whole movement more fruitful, for it has led to a constant process of testing, probing and exploring, all aimed at refining or redirecting the scope and operation of phenomenology.

Fortunately, it is not necessary for our present purpose to thread our way through all the many interpretations that have been developed, and we shall preface our study by simply noting the historical origin of the movement with Edmund Husserl and by introducing the three philosophers whose analyses of intersubjectivity are to be examined. The presentation of their views will itself serve to illustrate how differently phenomenologists have seen both the boundaries of the question of intersubjectivity and the meaning of the phenomenological method.

Edmund Husserl (1859–1938), a German university professor, was the founder of contemporary phenomenology. On that point most scholars would agree. But agreement seems almost to end there. For Husserl had no sooner set forth the new method of phenomenology than disputes arose about the proper limits and goal of the method. In fact, even Husserl's own understanding of the meaning of phenomenology underwent major changes during his long career. Only one feature seems to have remained relatively constant – his conviction that phenomenology was the method by which philosophy for the first time in its history could transform itself into a true science. His programmatic essay of 1910, *Philosophy as Rigorous Science,* sets forth this view in detail.

The essay begins with the opening statement, "From its earliest beginnings philosophy has claimed to be rigorous science," and continues: "During no period of its development has philosophy been capable of living up to this claim."[3] And, more emphatically: "I do not say that philosophy is an imperfect science; I say simply that it is not yet a science at all, that as science it has not yet begun."[4] Phenomenology was to change all this. But Husserl's initial expectations were never satisfactorily achieved. The longer he worked to establish the absolute rigor of the phenomenological method, the more problems he encountered, and the more changes he introduced into his own thinking. Thus, though the goal remained the same, the mode

[3] Husserl, *Philosophy as Rigorous Science,* (trans. Quentin Lauer), New York, Harper (Torchbook), 1965, p. 71.

[4] *Ibid.,* p. 73.

of achieving it changed, and so one cannot even speak of "Husserl's theory" without further qualifying it by specifying the period intended. Added to this is the fact that most of Husserl's early disciples disagreed with the direction he took in his later development. They worked in total independence from him and elaborated their own theories. And as the movement spread to France in the 1930–1940 decade, even more versions appeared. So it is almost true to say that there are as many theories of phenomenology as there are phenomenologists. This astonishing proliferation took place during Husserl's own lifetime. So, like Freud in similar circumstances, he found former students – or even students of students – using phenomenological method or publishing their own versions of it before the master had arrived at his own final formulation.

Because of the vast complexity thus generated in the fifty-year history of the movement, we shall not attempt to describe even the major sub-movements within it. Rather we shall simply indicate in very brief fashion how Husserl first arrived at the essentials of his method and later modified it. After that we shall identify the three or four points which most phenomenologists would seem to agree on. Later, as we introduce each of the three phenomenologists to be studied, Jean-Paul Sartre, Max Scheler and Dietrich von Hildebrand, we shall note briefly how their views differ from Husserl's.

Husserl came to philosophy – and phenomenology – by an indirect route. His academic training was in mathematics, with a dissertation on the functions of complex variables. His first book, *The Philosophy of Arithmetic* in 1891, was a contribution to the growing field of the foundations of mathematics. In it, Husserl attempted to explain basic mathematical concepts as the products of certain psychological acts of grouping and abstraction. One can suspect that he had perhaps succumbed to the temptation, then widespread, to re-interpret other disciplines in terms of the relatively new science of empirical psychology. In any case, Husserl's view was severely criticized by the famous theoretician Gottlieb Frege, whose own *Foundations of Arithmetic* (1884) had portrayed mathematics as a totally independent domain to which psychology could contribute nothing in the way of fundamental explanations.

Frege's sharp criticism appears to have been at least one of the factors that caused Husserl to do a complete about-face. He became convinced of the absoluteness of mathematical and logical entities and of their total independence from psychological acts. Then, as he slowly moved away from mathematics to philosophy, he became an outspoken foe of psychological reductionism in all areas of philosophy. Just as mathematical thinking had to be allotted its own domain of independent "objects" which were invariant meaning-structures, so Husserl came to feel that all modes of human experience must similarly contain their own specific invariant structures. These function as the a priori element of all meaningfulness in experience, and they cannot be explained away as the product of "merely psychological" acts.

These a priori structures of experience Husserl called "essences," and the mode by which they could be apprehended he spoke of as "intuition." In a sense, both terms were perhaps poor choices, since the notion of "intuiting essences" seemed to carry overtones more associated with mysticism than with the scientific rigor that Husserl was aiming at. But he defended the choice of terms as accurately expressing what he meant. "Intuiting essences conceals no more difficulties or 'mystical' secrets than does perception," he insists. "When we bring 'color' to full intuitive clarity, to givenness for ourselves, then the datum is an 'essence'; and when we likewise in pure intuition – looking, say, at one perception after another – bring to givenness for ourselves what 'perception' is, perception in itself (this identical character of any number of flowing singular perceptions), then we have intuitively grasped the essence of perception."[5]

Since these essential structures, though given in experience, are latent, and not immediately obvious, a new method is needed to discern them. The new method attempts to identify and to seize by intellectual intuition those constant elements that, by persisting unchanged through the manifold fluctuations of experience make experience itself an intelligible continuum. These identity-structures thus become the phenomena to be discovered and studied by the new philosophical method that Husserl called phenomenology. Prior to Husserl, of course, the term phenomenology had been primarily associated with Hegel and the term phenomena with Kant. And though Husserl is following neither Hegel nor Kant, there is at least a thin similarity in this respect: For all three, a phenomenon is that which is in some way given, and it does not have to be reached by a process of reasoning. They are not in agreement, however, on precisely what these phenomena are in the concrete.

Husserl consequently goes to considerable lengths to make it clear that what he means by phenomena is not to be equated with the Kantian "appearances" of things in the world. Nor, on the other hand, are the Husserlian phenomena to be interpreted as those details of inner experience that Hume studied by psychological introspection. "The whole thing," Husserl ex-

[5] *Ibid.*, p. 110–111.

plains, "depends on one's seeing and making entirely one's own the truth that just as immediately as one can hear a sound, so one can intuit an 'essence' – the essence 'sound,' the essence 'appearance of thing,' the essence 'apparition,' the essence 'pictorial representation,' the essence 'judgment' or 'will,' etc. – and in the intuition one can make an essential judgment. On the other hand, however, it depends on one's protecting himself from the Humean confusion and accordingly not confounding phenomenological intuition with 'introspection,' with interior experience – in short, with acts that posit not essences but individual details corresponding to them." [6]

Husserl used the term "description" to distinguish his new method from other philosophical approaches. Designating phenomenology as a "descriptive" science led to some confusion, though Husserl apparently meant only to emphasize that, unlike mathematics, it was not to be a deductive science.[7] Description is rather the name for that progressive intellectual intuition by which one isolates and identifies the "object," the essence or eidos, that phenomenology is concerned with, for, "phenomenology is not a science of fact but rather an apriori science of essences; more precisely, it is a science that investigates *essential types*." [8]

As Husserl continued his analysis of the various essential types identifiable in experience, however, his interest gradually shifted to a further question: What is the foundation for the absoluteness and invariance of the discovered essences? Husserl concluded that a suitable foundation could not be found in the unstable manifold of contingent fact, and that it must be located in the realm of consciousness itself. For such structural constants of experience would necessarily be ideal types unaffected by changing facts. And only consciousness could provide the matrix within which such idealized constants could be constituted.

Two major factors entered into Husserl's new concern. There was first his long-time interest in determining the being that pure meaning-structures can have. There was also his development of a theory of the intentionality of consciousness, a modified version of the old medieval view of intentionality. Central to Husserl's view was the notion that the essence of consciousness is "intending a meaning." Consciousness therefore was conceived as a

[6] *Ibid.*, p. 115.

[7] "Phenomenology is an apriori science, *but it is not deductive*. We believe it possible to affirm that it is this negativity that Husserl primarily meant to indicate by designating phenomenology as a descriptive science, i.e., phenomenology is called descriptive *because* it is not deductive." Susan Bachelard, *A Study of Husserl's Formal and Transcendental Logic,* (trans. Lester Embree) Evanston, Northwestern Univ. Press. 1968, p. xlvi.

[8] *Ibid.*, p. xlvi.

special kind of "medium" within which essences were constituted as invariant meanings. The empirical facts to which a single meaning might apply could vary in innumerable ways, but the unity of the meaning remained, its absoluteness guaranteeing the continuity and intelligibility of experience.

Against all simple empiricisms, consciousness was thus not a simple mirror of events. Rather, it was a unique intending medium, which, by intending a meaning, simultaneously endowed the invariant meaning with a peculiar kind of being, an absolute being, possible only in the realm of conscious being. For Husserl, as Lauer points out, "To speak of consciousness . . . is not to speak of the activity whereby a subject is conscious; it is to speak of a mode of being, the mode of being which things have when we are conscious of them."[9]

With this shift of interest from a simple inventory of essences to an explanation of their constitution in consciousness, Husserl seemed to his disciples to have abandoned the quest for a middle road between realism and idealism, and to have yielded to a form of idealism – a perennial temptation, apparently, for German philosophers. His earliest American commentator, Marvin Farber, points out that with his move toward phenomenological idealism, "Husserl has exceeded the limits of a purely descriptive philosophy."[10] Farber himself, like most of Husserl's early followers, regretted the idealistic turn, disagreed with Husserl's later attempts at a transcendental phenomenology with its Kantian-Cartesian overtones, and felt "compelled to reject the systematic attempts at its justification."[11]

The progressive development of Husserl's idealistic position is an incredibly involved one, and cannot be discussed here. We shall only note that among the gravest problems that beset his theory of the constitution of essential types of meaning within the matrix of consciousness, was the problem of how *another* human being, in all his individuality and specificity, could be constituted within my consciousness and yet be truly other to me. Husserl struggled with this problem of the intrasubjective constitution of the other subject in a number of his works; the most extensive treatment is given in the fifth meditation of his *Cartesian Meditations*. But even his most sympathetic followers have not found the explanation free from ambiguity. The whole topic of intersubjectivity in Husserl is so complex that it could be adequately discussed only within the context of a full discussion of his

[9] Quentin Lauer, *Phenomenology: Its Genesis and Prospect,* New York, Harper (Torchbook), 1965, p. 36.

[10] Marvin Farber, *The Foundation of Phenomenology,* Cambridge, Harvard Univ. Press, 1943, p. 566.

[11] *Ibid.*, p. vi.

phenomenology, and for that reason we omit any discussion of it in this book.[12] Since the three phenomenologists we examine do not adopt Husserl's idealistic viewpoint, the problem of the other person does not present itself as one of constitution within consciousness, as we shall see.

As Husserl had moved further and further into the involved problem of how a world of absolute essences could be constituted within the realm of conscious being, his original program of descriptive or "eidetic" phenomenology was being carried out, with various modifications, by a great number of other phenomenologists. Their researches covered a wide range of different phenomena. Thus, long before Husserl had elaborated his later Cartesian theory of intersubjectivity, scholars who had been inspired by his early "eidetic" theory had begun to apply the new method to the study of interpersonal relationships. In this area the names of Adolph Reinach, Max Scheler, and Dietrich von Hildebrand were prominent. Reinach (who died at an early age) had been trained in law and was especially concerned with the phenomenological analysis of the intersubjective bonds created by legal acts (contracts, etc.). Scheler and von Hildebrand studied ethical and other intersubjective phenomena in an effort to identify essential types of social acts and the intersubjective relationships they give rise to. With the exportation of phenomenology to France in the 1930–1940 period, the question of intersubjectivity was again reexamined by Sartre and others.

Meanwhile, variant forms of the method were spreading beyond philosophy into other disciplines, and as Husserl concentrated more and more on problems associated with the development of transcendental phenomenology, investigators in widely diverse fields were applying adaptations of the basic phenomenological insight – the search for invariant essences – to the most varied subject-matter.

> Unlike the investigations of Husserl, those of his followers range over a wide field, so that there is scarcely an aspect of philosophy or of science which has not been investigated phenomenologically. To mention but a few: we find that Heidegger, Jaspers, Sartre, Marcel, and Conrad-Martius are developing the phenomenological method in its ontological implications; Pfänder, Geiger, Merleau-Ponty, Ricoeur, and Binswanger apply it to psychology; Scheler, Von Hildebrand, and Hartmann have developed a phenomenological ethics and general theory of values; Otto, Hering, and Van de Leeuw have studied religion in the same way; while in esthetics Simmel, Ingarden, Malraux, Dufrenne, and Lipps

[12] Two studies of intersubjectivity in Husserl are now available in English: Paul Ricoeur, *Husserl: An Analysis of His Phenomenology,* Evanston, Northwestern Univ. Press, 1967, Chapter Five "Husserl's Fifth Cartesian Meditation." Alfred Schutz, "The Problem of Transcendental Intersubjectivity in Husserl," *Collected Papers of Alfred Schutz,* The Hague, Nijhoff, 1966, Vol. III, pp. 51–84.

have been conspicuously succesful. Among these same authors we find contributions to epistemological, sociological, linguistic, and logical developments. All are in one way or another concerned with the *essences* of the concepts employed in these disciplines.[13]

Because of the great variety of positions taken by phenomenologists, the different fields of interest they investigate, and the freedom of approach which the method seems intrinsically to allow, one may well wonder if there could be any common core accepted by all. Spiegelberg, at the end of his two-volume study of the movement, has attempted to identify such a core.[14] He finds only two major features: The first is the general agreement that phenomenology is a method, not a system. The second is an acceptance of three methodical steps which "have been accepted, at least implicitly, and practiced by all those who have aligned themselves with the phenomenological movement."[15] The three commonly accepted steps: "investigating particular phenomena, investigating general essences, and apprehending essential relationships among essences."[16] Beyond that, wide differences exist.

In the face of such limited agreement about the central features of the method itself, it is not surprising to find that the topic of intersubjectivity has been analyzed in very different fashion by a number of phenomenologists. The three views presented in this book reflect that diversity. All three profess to study the human subject in his intersubjective situation and yet they come to vastly different conclusions. If we were to characterize each view in one word, we might say that the first is a phenomenology of loneliness, the second a phenomenology of life, and the third a phenomenology of love. Sartre denies that subject-to-subject relationships are possible and thus sees the subject's basic situation as that of ontological loneliness. Scheler, on the contrary finds men essentially and inescapably social because all share a common and universal life-stream. Von Hildebrand sees man forging bonds of community with others by reason of his power of transcending self through love. We shall say a word of introduction about each before beginning a detailed examination of their views.

"Hell is – other people," says a character in one of Sartre's plays. The phrase is not intended merely as a startling dramatic line. Sartre has composed a complete ontology that defends the proposition as literal truth. For

[13] Lauer, *op. cit.*, p. 4.

[14] Herbert Spiegelberg, *The Phenomenological Movement,* The Hague, Nijhoff, 2 vols., 1965, Vol. II, Chap. XIV, "The Essentials of the Method," pp. 653–701.

[15] *Ibid.*, p. 659.

[16] *Ibid.*, p. 659.

in the course of his phenomenology of being, he has proposed the most completely elaborated denial of true intersubjectivity that has ever appeared in philosophy. His phenomenology has been called a philosophy of the free human person. More correctly, however, it could be described as a philosophy of isolation. For it denies the very possibility of all positive intersubjective relationships, either with other persons or with a transcendent being.

Such a philosophy is both a-social and a-theistic; indeed, Sartre has declared with keen insight that it is the only logical consequence of a real atheism. It denies that man's ontological status can be thought of as one of creaturehood; rather, man is "God-in-the-making," for man's destiny is to strive forever to become "God" (in Sartre's odd sense) and forever to fail in the attempt.

This theory of the inevitability of failure in life reveals another foundation stone of Sartrean existentialism. Not only is it a philosophy of isolation, but it is equally a "philosophy of the absurd." Its basic tenet is that both man and the universe are completely irrational, inexplicable, absurd. Whereas other philosophies throughout history, had always claimed to explain man and his universe, this new ontology proposes exactly the opposite. The Greeks had sought to give the logos for each thing; for Sartre the true one can know who man is and what position he holds in the universe; the logos is precisely this, that there is no logos. Wisdom had always meant that new wisdom is to know that man can never know what he is, where he came from, or why he is here. Man finds himself a castaway in a world which he cannot fathom because it is irrational, in a world in which he must nevertheless continually exercise his power of free choice to "make" himself. By what norm should he guide his choice? There is no norm. What then should he choose? Anything – since all choices are equally absurd, the content of the choice does not matter; all that is imposed on man is the necessity of choice; even in not choosing, he has already chosen.

What then constitutes the "good" life for the Sartrean man? There is no really "good" life; there is only an "authentic" one. The authentic life consists in facing squarely the absurdity of existence, and even in the face of this, choosing freely to make one's future. To attempt to escape from the absurdity of the world is to be unauthentic; to find counterfeit solace in any "system" which transcends the isolated individual, or in some imagined communion with another subject, this too is to be unauthentic. The Sartrean "authentic man" is the very apotheosis of the "tough-minded man."[17]

[17] The psychoanalysts were not slow to interpret the philosophy of Sartre as a reflection of his psychological problems. Emmanuel Mounier, *op. cit.,* p. 81 ff., finds the syndrome of the paranoid; Peter Dempsey, *The Psychology* of Sartre, Westminster,

Not only does Sartre isolate man from a transcendent God and leave him abandoned in an irrational world, but he denies the person even the possibility of lessening his misery by communion with another human being. Coincident with the irrationality of the world comes the complete objectification of the human subject. There is here a bizarre distortion of the insight of Kierkegaard regarding the importance of subjectivity. For we have now subjectivity locked within itself.

It is clear that Sartre does not see philosophy as a mere academic discipline. He does not confine himself to analyzing for hundreds of pages some mysterious vacuity that he calls "nothingness." His philosophy is not only intended as a strange new ontology; it lays equal claim to be a new ethic for human living, a total way of life as far-reaching in its precepts as is any religious way of life. Sartre himself has defended his view as a complete "humanism" free from the outmoded trappings of the old God-centered philosophies. And in his most recent work, *The Critique of Dialectical Reason,* the new humanism finds its logical extension in a new social philosophy, a modified Marxism. The latest comprehensive study of Sartre's ontology emphasizes the close link between the early ontology and the current Sartrean social philosophy. Klaus Hartmann, discussing the development of Sartre's thought, points out that "with the appearance of the new book on the dialectic of reason the position taken in his preceding works stands forth as completed. Sartre has not abandoned the position taken in these [early] works, but rather extends it to cover a social philosophy under the auspices of a Marxist orientation."[18]

Max Scheler, the phenomenologist of intersubjectivity whose views are examined in Section Two, is not as well known in the English-speaking world as is Sartre; the translation of his works has progressed very slowly. But Scheler was one of the most brilliant figures in German phenomenological circles during the first three decades of the century. His writings cover almost every field in philosophy, but all are written from a certain unified perspective. This stems from the fact that Scheler's prime concern was the human person in his various existential relations with other persons. This absorbing interest in the subject's living ties with other subjects runs through all of Scheler's works on ethics, philosophy of religion, sociology of knowledge, emotional life, metaphysics and theory of knowledge.

Like Kierkegaard, Scheler saw philosophy radiating out from the study

Md., Newman, 1950, pp. 22–24; 55–60, traces the difficulty to parental rejection; S. Naesgaard, "Le Complexe de Sartre," *Psyche,* 3, 1948, pp. 655–665, also relates Sartre's attitude of hostility to childhood maladjustments.

[18] Klaus Hartmann, *Sartre's Ontology,* Evanston, Northwestern Univ. Press, 1966, p. xiii.

of human subjectivity. Unlike Sartre, he saw man as an "open" being – open to the world and to other subjects. Man, for Scheler, is so destined for life with others that the social dimension is an a priori structure of his being. He is born into a social reality, and though he emerges as an individual, he can never sever the ontological ties binding him to others. Scheler's emphasis on social context as all-encompassing led him to postulate a form of panvitalism in his ultimate explanation of intersubjectivity. As we shall see, his ultimate position appears as extreme a statement on intersubjectivity as is Sartre's, but at the opposite extreme.

In a sense, many of Scheler's studies represent an attempt to incorporate the results of modern psychological research with the new method of phenomenology. Trained during the golden era of the older school of German psychology, Scheler was keenly aware of its limitations, and hailed the movement of self-criticism within psychological circles which aimed at establishing that discipline with a greater orientation toward the total human person. Despite his enthusiasm for the new approach to philosophy which phenomenology promised, Scheler was not limited to accepting as dogma the various limitations and restrictions which Husserl had imposed on the method. He culled from it those features which would assist him in a detailed and rigorous analysis of the person and his existential relations.

Unsuited by temperament to the step-by-step progress of Husserl, Scheler was more in the Augustinian, Pascalian tradition. Like Kierkegaard he stressed the existential human situation and his writings reveal how deeply he attempted to understand it. Scheler's work, therefore, is no mere mechanical synthesis of psychology and phenomenology; it bears the stamp of his original genius. The person in his human situation which Scheler describes from many points of view was not an abstraction but the willing, thinking, feeling person of actual life. Scheler never lost sight of the fact that the proper subject for a philosophy of man was not the cartesian abstraction of thought and extension, but the concrete existent, the "incarnate person."

The third philosopher in our study, von Hildebrand, had like Scheler, subscribed to the original eidetic phenomenology of Husserl, seeing in it a method for the development of a contemporary realism. But, as with many other early disciples he parted company with the master when Husserl began to move toward a more idealistic position. Von Hildebrand is more emphatic than Scheler in stressing the reality and objectivity of the phenomena he analyzes. Especially in recent years, with the growing scholarly interest in Husserl's transcendental phenomenology with its Cartesian overtones, von Hildebrand has been at pains to distinguish his position from

Husserl's, and to point up his realism. In his study of intersubjective relationships he feels he is dealing with facts that are ontologically real and objective. Since he had never embraced Husserl's transcendental idealism, he is not faced in his study of intersubjectivity with Husserl's problem of justifying how one Cartesian-type subject can reach another.

Rather, because of his objective realism, he considers the intersubjective relationships between persons and the human acts by which such relationships arise to be included in the immediate given, and thus to be entirely legitimate objects for phenomenological consideration. Von Hildebrand is well aware that many philosophers, especially in the Anglo-American tradition, would consider these acts to be "merely subjective psychological states" and of no ontological relevance. Part of the difficulty, he feels, arises because of the connotations of the word "subjective," as applied to such human acts and relationships. "For many people, even for certain philosophers, the term 'subjective' even when it refers to such objective realities as acts of will and joy, or to the person himself, connotes something less real . . . which exists only in the 'mind' of a person – a mere reality *in mente.*"[19] But for von Hildebrand, such states-of-affairs as human attitudes and acts, community-bonds, and values, all possess at least as much reality and objectivity as physical things.

Partly through the influence of Scheler and partly because of his basic Augustinian orientation, von Hildebrand has devoted himself almost exclusively to the analysis of ethical, social and interpersonal situations. His work shows intense concern for the existential individual and painstaking care in the description of the fine nuances of intersubjective relationships. He provides an elaborate analysis of the various modes of human community extending from simple two-person relationships up through the larger social units in which the individual is incorporated. For von Hildebrand, man's social relationships are essential and a priori, so that man is a genuinely social being, but he finds no phenomenological justification for grounding man's social a priori in a panvitalism as Scheler proposes. His analysis of the intersubjective situation thus represents an interesting challenge to the two others examined here.

It need not be emphasized, of course, that no one of the three views discussed in this book is presented as any kind of final answer to the question of intersubjectivity. Rather, one might hope that the very diversity exhibited in this brief sampling of European phenomenological thought on the problem would serve as an introduction to the complexities of the whole topic and help to stimulate new thinking along new lines.

[19] Dietrich von Hildebrand, *What is Philosophy?*, Milwaukee, Bruce, 1960, p. 154.

SECTION ONE

JEAN-PAUL SARTRE
THE PHENOMENOLOGY OF LONELINESS

CHAPTER I

SUBJECTIVITY IN SARTRE

Jean-Paul Sartre is unquestionably the best known French philosopher since Bergson. He is also one of the most productive – novels, plays, essays and huge philosophical tomes testify to an unflagging zeal. He has written on topics ranging from psychoanalysis to Marxism. But through all his work, however diverse in form and content, there is a certain unity – a unity of perspective with regard to the nature of man. From his early writings until his latest, Sartre's basic concept of man has remained essentially unchanged, though it has been progressively elaborated. This understanding of what human subjectivity means underlies not only his philosophical works, but his literary and dramatic writings as well. It is this fundamental theme – Sartre's notion of the human subject and his intersubjective relationships – that we shall be discussing in this section. The Sartrean view of intersubjectivity can be found expressed in many of his plays and novels. Our examination of it, however, will be made solely from his philosophical writings where he has given a detailed presentation in the technical language of phenomenology.

Sartre's phenomenological heritage is a broad one, for he has been influenced not only by Husserl, but also by the writings of Heidegger, Hegel, and Marx. With his own fertile genius working on these rich sources, Sartre has produced several major philosophical works that are impressive even to those who disagree with his conclusions.[1] Because of its uniqueness,

[1] Thus, Gabriel Marcel, the French theistic existentialist who vigorously opposes the Sartrean philosophy, was quick to admit the importance of it. "I believe the importance of this view should not be underestimated. This was a point of difference between me and some of my colleagues at the Sorbonne toward the end of 1943; I was told that I worried too much ... But I believed then, as I do now, that Sartre's philosophy was much too impressive, particularly to young people, not to be examined with the utmost seriousness and objectivity." Gabriel Marcel, *The Philosophy of Existentialism,* trans. Manya Harari, New York, Citadel, 5th ed., 1965, p. 48.

Sartre's phenomenology is not easily compared with previous ones, either the realistic viewpoint of the earlier German thinkers or the more idealistic perspective of the later Husserl. He sees phenomenology as geared neither to realism nor to idealism but as transcending both in a most unusual way. Consequently he emphasizes certain methodological procedures and ignores others. For example, his work contains extremely well done phenomenological descriptions of the kind associated with eidetic phenomenology. But he does not limit himself to the intuitive description of essences. He draws on certain idealistic themes in Husserl's later work and drastically modifies them. In addition, he also utilizes a kind of Hegelian and Marxist dialectic, a genuine novelty in phenomenological technique.

Despite his technical knowledge of various phenomenological approaches, however, and his versatility in welding selected procedures into his new method, Sartre's major concern has never been the intramural disputes of methodology. It has rather been the analysis of man in his existential situation. This has led him to elaborate a complete and highly distinctive phenomenology of the human being in his *total* social situation, embracing the purely intersubjective, the political and the economic dimensions.

Toward the completion of this project Sartre has already produced two lengthy and dense philosophical treatises. The first, *Being and Nothingness*[2] (1943) sets forth an extraordinary phenomenological ontology in which the subject and his intersubjective relationships are totally reinterpreted in a highly original way. The second book, *Critique of Dialectical Reason*[3] (1960) starts from the base provided by his new philosophy of the subject and builds on it a broad social theory of a modified Marxism. But, though accepting some economic and social categories of Marxism, Sartre has not embraced the militant materialism typically associated with its theoretical foundations. "I am neither materialist nor spiritualist. I part with dialectical materialism, in this sense, that according to my view (1) man has goals which matter does not have, (2) and man has a choice of possibilities which matter does not have."[4] Sartre thus appears to be as eclectic in his Marxism as he is in his phenomenology.

Our examination of Sartre's views on intersubjectivity will be concerned

[2] Jean-Paul Sartre, *Being and Nothingness,* trans. Hazel Barnes, New York, Philosophical Library, 1965. A translation of *L'Être et le Néant,* Paris, Gallimard, 1943. The Barnes translation will be given in the text, with the French original in the footnotes. The English translation will be cited as *BN,* the French as *EN.*

[3] Jean-Paul Sartre, *Critique de la Raison Dialectique,* Paris, 1960.

[4] Wilfred Desan, *The Tragic Finale,* New York, Harper, (Torchbook) rev. ed., 1960, p. xvi. Desan is quoting from an interview he had with Sartre in 1956.

principally with the first of his two works, *Being and Nothingness*, in which he sets forth the general theory of the possibility and limits of intersubjective relationships. After we have discussed this, we shall indicate briefly how the later social theory develops within the previously set limits.

Sartre encountered phenomenology at first hand during a study-year (1933–34) in Germany. He seems to have been equally impressed by Husserl and by Heidegger. The latter, a former assistant to Husserl, had never subscribed to the master's idealism, but had himself developed a phenomenology of human existence as a prelude to a general phenomenological ontology. His first book, *Being and Time,*[5] (1927) was widely acclaimed, and Heidegger seemed to many to have wisely avoided Husserl's endless analyses of the Ego and consciousness and to have pointed out a more fruitful path that phenomenology should take. Sartre drew inspiration from both thinkers. His *Being and Nothingness* is similar to Heidegger's *Being and Time* in presenting an ontology of human existence, but it utilizes a method that combines elements from Husserl and Hegel as well. References to all three philosophers are numerous throughout the book, and Sartre frequently uses them as the opposition against which his own views are set forth.

That Heidegger's work should have served as the inspiration for Sartre's development of what has come to be called "existential" phenomenology is somewhat ironic. For in turning phenomenological scrutiny away from essences given in consciousness and toward the structures of human existence, Heidegger was not proposing to develop an existential phenomenology as such. He intended his analysis of the structures of "subjectivity" or "existence" (as Kierkegaard had named man's special mode of being) to be simply the first step toward a general ontology. He was most emphatic in pointing out that his concern lay not with the preliminary analysis of man's being but with the general theory of being he was developing. But the extraordinary depth and richness of Heidegger's description of the structures of human existence in *Being and Time* drew attention away from his more ultimate goal of a general ontology. And the failure of Heidegger to publish such a general ontology added to the impression that his work represented principally an important new phenomenological development – existential phenomenology.

Actually, many of Husserl's early disciples had been doing a kind of

[5] Martin Heidegger, *Being and Time,* trans. John Macquarrie and Edward Robinson, N.Y., Harper and Row, 1962. Translation of *Sein und Zeit,* originally published in 1927, in *Jahrbuch für Philosophie und phänomenologische Forschung* (Halle), VIII, 1–438.

existential phenomenology long before the name was coined and even before Heidegger's *Being and Time* appeared. Scheler, Reinach, von Hildebrand and others had focused their phenomenological analyses almost entirely on the existing person and his interpersonal relationships in the ethical and social realms. Though it lacked the specific Kierkegaardian theme of anguished existence, this work could be called existential phenomenology in a broad sense. But with Heidegger and Sartre the category of existence becomes more thematic and we find extensive phenomenological descriptions of the structural dimensions of existence through the categories of dread, care, resolution, temporality, finitude, freedom and decision.

The Sartrean analysis of existence, however, is as different from Heidegger's as the Sartrean phenomenology is different from Husserl's. For Sartre never borrows – he radically transforms. This became evident in the initial statement of his phenomenological views given by Sartre in 1936 in *The Transcendence of the Ego*. In this short work he had a twofold aim. First he launched a devastating critique of that most central presupposition of Husserl's later phenomenology – the theory of the transcendental Ego. Then he proposed a substitute theory of his own, on which his later work, *Being and Nothingness* is based. The total effect is to produce a new version of phenomenology that has some resemblance to Husserl's project but differs vastly from it. Since an understanding of how Sartre modified Husserl's view is essential for an appreciation of the Sartrean notion of subjectivity, we shall indicate briefly here the new perspective that Sartre introduces.

During his studies in Germany, Sartre had encountered the later Husserl who was principally concerned at that time with explaining how essences were constituted in the realm of conscious being generated by the Ego. Great difficulties beset Husserl's attempts to explain the relationship between Ego and consciousness, for it would seem that the Ego must simultaneously be totally immersed in consciousness and yet transcendent to it in order to be able to reflect on the structures of consciousness. Husserl was driven to postulating several "layers" of Ego, a procedure which appeared only to involve even more insoluble problems.

Faced with this tangle of hypotheses, Sartre proposed a simple, but drastic solution. He denied outright the most basic Husserlian presupposition – that the Ego is given as the most primary phenomenon – and thus dissolved the entire problem. Husserl had always assumed that the most unquestioned and unquestionable phenomenon was the fact that we are immediately aware of a consciousness-radiating Ego. This was the *primary* phenomenological fact. Given that, we could then observe how essential structures came to be constituted in consciousness.

Sartre denies that consciousness of the Ego is the primary fact. The Ego, he points out, is a structure *in* consciousness. Therefore like all structures it is a product of consciousness and not the source of it. "The Ego is not the owner of consciousness; it is the *object* of consciousness,"[6] he insists. Consciousness as such is simply an *impersonal intentional awareness*. After a long dissection of Husserl's view and a presentation of his own Sartre concludes. "We may therefore formulate our thesis: transcendental consciousness is an impersonal spontaneity."[7]

Where Husserl, and Descartes before him, had posited the thinking Ego as the primary fact, Sartre proposes that the Ego arises only through reflection. He points to the fact that in immediate unreflective experience we are totally absorbed in the object. We are not aware of ourselves as an Ego but only as an awareness intending an object. More properly therefore, Descartes should have said "*There is* consciousness of this object," rather than "I *have* consciousness of this object," if he wished to describe the most primary conscious fact. For prior to Descartes' Cogito (the reflective "I think") there is, in Sartre's terminology, the pre-reflexive Cogito, the pure impersonal conscious existing. Only in reflective consciousness does the Ego-structure arise, for we have then moved from sheer consciousness.[8]

Sartre's astonishing proposal has two major consequences: By denying that the transcendental Ego either generates consciousness or constitutes essences within consciousness, Sartre undercuts the possibility of any idealism and makes it appear that Husserl's idealistic problems were those of his own making. For if there is no Ego living in the world of its own ideas there can be no idealism. The result, as we shall see, is to bring Sartre close to an unusual kind of "realism" – if such traditional categories have any validity in such a changed perspective.

[6] J.-P. Sartre, *The Transcendence of the Ego,* trans. Forrest Williams and Robert Kirkpatrick, New York, Noonday, 1957, p. 97.

[7] *Ibid.,* p. 98.

[8] The difficulties of interpreting the Sartrean non-Ego theory of consciousness, from out of which, nevertheless, the Ego arises as an objective structure, have led to a basic disagreement between the two best known American interpreters of Sartre. Thus, Desan, (*The Tragic Finale,* p. 144, sq.) feels that once Sartre has "banished the Ego" as the font of consciousness he cannot legitimately re-introduce an Ego with personal identity in the later discussions of intersubjectivity. Barnes, on the contrary (Translator's Introduction of *Being and Nothingness,* p. xxxvii) feels that Sartre intends to say that each pre-reflexive Cogito is always from the beginning an individual and particular one that builds a unified personality through its own choices. The reflexive act then objectifies this unity to bring the Ego before consciousness as an object.

A second consequence of the non-Ego theory of consciousness is Sartre's novel and somewhat paradoxical theory of being. As we shall see, Sartre's new ontology is difficult to discuss because although he uses traditional concepts and categories he intends them in a radically non-traditional sense. This is especially true of his treatment of the being of the conscious subject and his subsequent analysis of intersubjectivity. In highly condensed terms, Sartre's views might be expressed in this fashion: Since primary consciousness is not to be thought of as arising from an Ego-subject, but rather is the sheer spontaneous and Ego-less "intending" of an object, then it is more proper to designate consciousness as a "nothing" rather than as a "something". In other words, we should think of consciousness more as an open aperture in being than as a being itself.

This notion of each consciousness as a tiny "nothingness" in the midst of massive, overwhelming nonconscious being supplies the title for Sartre's best known work, *Being and Nothingness*. In it he presents a phenomenology of the human subject as the conscious being whose very meaning is to introduce nothingness into being. If we were to use the noun "nothing" as an active *verb* then we would come close to Sartre's meaning by saying that "Man nothings". And this spontaneous upwelling of man's "nothing-ing" (the participle of our new verb!) is his existence, and it appears as an invasion of that realm of non-conscious being that encompasses him.

Sartre's new ontology thus poses a dualism of nonconscious and conscious being (or, being and nothingness). How fruitful will the new ontology be? Has Sartre, perhaps without realizing it, simply found his way out of the bewildering fog of German speculation back to the familiar clime of classical French philosophy, where two great modes of being – Descartes called them mind and matter – stand in clear, distinct, and perpetual opposition to each other because they have been dialectically defined in relation to each other? Or has Sartre come upon a genuinely new and productive conception of being? It is perhaps too soon to decide such a question. In any case, he has effectively challenged Husserlian idealism and established to his own satisfaction a foundation for the phenomenological ontology to be set forth in *Being and Nothingness*. In this work, all being is now seen as belonging to these two major types – sheer consciousness that "intends" objects and structures itself into the Ego, and over against this, non-conscious being. By a kind of "dialectical" phenomenology, as we shall see, Sartre finds both types revealing themselves simultaneously.

He then directs his phenomenological intuition toward this newly disclosed realm of being and thus institutes a phenomenological ontology. But it is not so much a general ontology (Heidegger's goal) as it is an ontology of existence, of that special mode of being that only conscious being possesses. And thus it can correctly be said that Sartre is principally concerned with elaborating an existential phenomenology. After his analysis of human existence Sartre then explores the possibility and limits of existential intersubjectivity. We shall begin, therefore, by examining how Sartre arrives at his new concept of the human subject. In the next chapter we shall explore his phenomenology of intersubjectivity.

The Dialectical Disclosure of Being

When Sartre published in 1943 the comprehensive statement of his phenomenology of existence in the massive volume entitled *Being and Nothingness*, he added the sub-title "An Essay on Phenomenological Ontology." He regards his work as the first outline of a new ontology which will embrace a complete theory of being in general and of man in particular. In intention – as in size – the work is of epic proportions. Sartre sees himself the prophet of another Copernican revolution in philosophy, sketching the plan of a new ontology.[9] Were the new ontology of Sartre more similar to the old, we might pass it by and proceed directly to Sartre's notion of the subject. But Sartre's ontology is unlike anything which has yet appeared under that title, and his notion of subject is consequently just as unique and unprecedented. Sartre's theory of man and intersubjectivity is understandable only when we see its direct derivation from the fundamental categories of the new ontology. For this reason we shall outline briefly the "transcendental deduction" which Sartre employs to arrive at the two basic types of being, being-in-itself and being-for-itself.

Prefixed to Sartre's study of being and nothingness is a lengthy and dense introduction aimed at establishing the existence of the in-itself as opposed to the for-itself, or being of consciousness. The distinction of these two basic types of being provides the structure for the entire ontology of Sartre. Curiously enough, as we shall see, once Sartre has established the existence of the in-itself, almost nothing more can be said about it. "It is" – this is the limit of our knowledge of it. The very nature of the in-itself prohibits us from analyzing it further. After thirty pages which establish the existence of the in-itself most of the more than seven hundred

[9] The most recent study of Sartre's ontology is one that emphasizes the Hegelian influence in the development of Sartre's categories of being: Klaus Hartmann, *Sartre's Ontology,* Evanston, Northwestern U. Press, 1966. Earlier studies include: D. Dubarle, "L'Ontologie phénoménologique," *Revue de philosophie* (1946), 90–123, and M. Natanson, *A Critique of Jean-Paul Sartre's Ontology,* "University of Nebraska Studies," 1951.

pages of *Being and Nothingness* are devoted to describing the for-itself, its structures, its projects and its checks.

Sartre first wishes to establish the existence of the two forms of being. His method of procedure yields both simultaneously. By an analysis of consciousness and the phenomenal data of consciousness, he finds that there is a reciprocal necessity involved whereby the transphenomenal nature of consciousness, requires that there be a transphenomenal being of phenomena, and vice versa. The analysis has two major parts:

1. As a first step in achieving this reduction, Sartre declares that analysis of phenomenon qua phenomenon reveals that it cannot be merely a reflection of something hidden behind itself. The error of Kant was to posit beyond the phenomenon an unknowable noumenon. The solution of Sartre is to declare that the phenomenon itself has a being, which will be the starting point for an analysis. "If the essence of the appearance is an 'appearing,' which is no longer opposed to any *being*, there arises a legitimate problem concerning *the being of this appearing*." [10]

This "being of the appearing" cannot itself be another phenomenon, since it is the very condition of the phenomenon itself. Therefore we may say that the "being of the phenomenon" is "transphenomenal." But here again we must avoid a Kantian interpretation. To say that the being of the phenomenon is transphenomenal is not to say that it is a noumenon behind the phenomenon, for "the first consequence of the 'theory of the phenomenon' is that the appearance does not refer to being as Kant's phenomenon refers to the noumenon. Since there is nothing behind the appearance, and since it indicates only itself (and the total series of appearances), it can not be *supported* by any being other than its own. The appearance can not be the thin film of nothingness which separates the being-of-the-subject from absolute-being." [11]

Thus our analysis reveals that the phenomenon possesses a being which is not itself similarly phenomenal, but rather transphenomenal. "In a word," says Sartre "the phenomenon of being is 'ontological' in the sense that we speak of the *ontological* proof of St. Anselm and Descartes. It is an appeal to being; it requires as phenomenon, a foundation which is trans-

[10] *BN*, p. xlviii. "Si l'essence de l'apparition est un *'paraître'* qui ne s'oppose plus à aucun *être*, il y a un problème légitime de *l'être de ce paraître*." *EN*, p. 14.

[11] *BN*, p. xlviii. "... la première conséquence de la 'théorie du phénomène,' c'est que l'apparition ne renvoie pas à l'être comme le phénomène kantien de noumène. Puisqu'il n'y a rien derrière elle et qu'elle n'indique qu'elle-même (et la série totale des apparitions), elle ne peut *être supportée* par un autre être que le sien propre, elle ne saurait être la mince pellicule de néant qui sépare l'être-sujet de l'être-absolu." *EN*, p. 14.

phenomenal. The phenomenon of being requires the transphenomenality of being."[12]

2. Not only is the being of phenomenon transphenomenal, but consciousness itself is also transphenomenal. Sartre demonstrates this as follows. All consciousness is *consciousness of* something. The very nature of consciousness is to be intentional or positional. Concomitant with all consciousness *of* something, however, there must be a primary consciousness of being consciousness. If this were not so, there would be no consciousness. "This is a necessary condition," Sartre points out, "for if my consciousness were not consciousness of being consciousness of the table, it would then be consciousness of that table without consciousness of being so. In other words, it would be a consciousness ignorant of itself, an unconscious – which is absurd."[13] Thus, he feels, we reach the conclusion that the being of consciousness must be as transphenomenal as the being of the phenomenon.

This primary consciousness is what Sartre calls "the prereflexive cogito" or non-thetic consciousness. Its essential characteristic is that it exhibits no duality. "Consciousness of self is not dual," Sartre emphasizes. "If we wish to avoid an infinite regress, there must be an immediate, non-cognitive relation of the self to itself."[14] This non-thetic awareness, therefore, cannot be reduced to a kind of reflective knowledge in which the object-subject duality is present. It is not consciousness of self as an object distinct from the subject.

Having established the pre-reflexive cogito, Sartre is now in a position to prove that the transphenomenal nature of pure consciousness prohibits the being of the phenomenon from reduction to a phenomenon whose existence depends on the subjective consciousness. He has already avoided the Kantian position of the unknowable noumenon by posing the special transphenomenal nature of the being of the phenomenon; Sartre hopes now to rescue the being of the phenomenon from the subjectivism of Berkeley's position. He does this by proving that this being of the phenomenon is re-

[12] *BN,* p. xlix. "En un mot, le phénomène d'être est 'ontologique' au sens où l'on appelle *ontologique* la preuve de saint Anselme et de Descartes. Il est un appel d'être; il exige, en tant que phénomène, un fondement qui soit transphénoménal. Le phénomène d'être exige la transphénoménalité de l'être." *EN,* p. 16.

[13] *BN,* p. iii. "C'est une condition nécessaire: si ma conscience n'était pas conscience d'être conscience de table, elle serait donc conscience de cette table sans avoir conscience de l'être ou, si l'on veut, une conscience qui s'ignorerait soi-même, une conscience inconsciente – ce qui est absurde." *EN,* p. 18.

[14] *BN,* p. lii. "La conscience de soi n'est pas couple. Il faut, si nous voulons éviter la régression à l'infini qu'elle soit rapport immédiat et non cognitif de soi à soi." *EN,* p. 19.

quired by the transphenomenality of the being of consciousness. "We are going to see . . . that this very transphenomenality requires that of the being of the phenomenon."[15] This is what he calls the "ontological proof."[16]

First we posit what has been established concerning the intentional nature of consciousness. "Consciousness is consciousness *of* something. This means that transcendence is the constitutive structure of consciousness; that is, that consciousness is born *supported* by a being which is not itself."[17] Secondly we juxtapose what has been established concerning the nature of pure consciousness. "What can properly be called subjectivity is consciousness (of) consciousness:"[18] Now this non-thetic consciousness, as we have seen, is pure unity, undifferentiated awareness. When it becomes qualified, therefore, it cannot be qualified by itself, but only by something other than self, or in other words, by a being which is transphenomenal. Sartre puts it as follows:

> But this consciousness (of being) consciousness must be qualified in some way, and it can be qualified only as revealing intuition or it is nothing. Now a revealing intuition implies something revealed. Absolute subjectivity can be established only in the face of something revealed; immanence can be defined only within the apprehension of a transcendent . . . . Consciousness implies in its being a non-conscious and transphenomenal being.[19]

Thus, says Sartre, we have started from pure appearance and arrived at full being. Consciousness has yielded a being beyond itself which is revealed to consciousness as something other than self and possessing a transphenomenal character. Sartre feels justified in applying to consciousness somewhat the same definition which Heidegger had reserved for the *Dasein;* he adds to it, however, to include the revelatory function of con-

[15] *BN,* p. lx. "Nous allons voir . . . que cette transphénoménalité même exige celle de l'être du phénomène." *EN,* p. 27.

[16] For a penetrating analysis of Sartre's attempt to establish the transphenomenality of being, see James Collins, "The existentialism of Jean-Paul Sartre," *Thought,* 23 (1949), 59–100.

[17] *BN,* p. lxi. "La conscience est conscience *de* quelque chose: cela signifie que la transcendance est structure constitutive de la conscience: c'est-à-dire que la conscience naît *portée* d'un être qui n'est pas elle." *EN,* p. 28.

[18] *BN,* p. lxi. "Ce qu'on peut nommer proprement subjectivité, c'est la conscience (de) conscience." *EN,* p. 28.

[19] *BN,* p. lxi. ". . . il faut que cette conscience (d'être) conscience se qualifie en quelque façon et elle ne peut se qualifier que comme intuition révélante, sinon elle n'est rien. Or, une intuition révélante implique un révélé. La subjectivité absolue ne peut se constituer qu'en face d'un révélé, l'immanence ne peut se définir que dans la saisie d'un transcendent. . . . la conscience implique dans son être un être non conscient et transphénoménal." *EN,* p. 29.

sciousness. "Consciousness is a being such that in its being, its being is in question in so far as this being implies a being other than itself."[20]

At last we have established the existence of being in-itself. It is the being revealed by consciousness, the "being of the phenomenon." Sartre again warns that it is not to be confused with a Kantian noumenon:

> We must understand that this being is no other than the transphenomenal being of phenomena and not a noumenal being which is hidden behind them. It is the being of this table, of this package of tobacco, of the lamp, more generally the being of the world which is implied by consciousness. It requires simply that the being of that which *appears* does not exist *only* in so far as it appears. The transphenomenal being of what exists *for consciousness* is itself *in itself*.[21]

Although, as we have said above, the in-itself does not admit of analysis, Sartre appends a brief description of what he means by it. We may note three characteristics:

1) Being-in-itself can never in any case act on consciousness; thus there is no possibility of a realistic solution to the problem of the relations of the two fundamental types of being. Neither, on the other hand, can consciousness have generated the in-itself; thus there is eliminated the idealistic solution to the problem.

2) Being-in-itself is not created. Creation *ex nihilo* cannot explain the emergence of the in-itself. For if it were conceived within a divine subjectivity it would always remain a mode of the intrasubjective being of the divine subject; and if the in-itself were thought of as posited outside the divine subjectivity, *à là* Leibniz, it would necessarily be conceived of as independent of divinity and opposed to it. The conclusion for Sartre is that the in-itself must be thought of as uncreated. This, however, does not mean that such being creates itself, for this would require that it be prior to itself.

3) Being-in-itself, therefore, is best described rather than defined and this is what Sartre does. In one word, being is *itself*. Thus it should not be thought of as either active or passive. Both of these categories are human constructs and refer to human conduct or the instruments of human conduct. Activity means that a conscious subject utilizes means in view of an

[20] *BN*, p. lxii. "La conscience est un être pour lequel il est dans son être question de son être et tant que cet être implique un être autre que lui." *EN*, p. 29.

[21] *BN*, p. lxii. "Il est bien entendu que cet être n'est autre que l'être transphénoménal des phénomènes, et non être nouménal qui se cacherait derrière eux. C'est l'être de cette table, de ce paquet de tabac, de la lampe, plus généralement l'être du monde qui est impliqué par la conscience. Elle exige simplement que l'être de ce qui *apparaît* n'existe pas *seulement* en tant qu'il apparaît. L'être transphénoménal de ce qui est *pour la conscience* est lui-même *en soi*." *EN*, p. 29.

end. Passivity describes the nature of the means we use insofar as they do not spontaneously direct themselves to the end we have in view. Thus, man alone can be called active, and the means he uses are passive. But these two concepts, abstracted from a human situation, lose all significance according to Sartre. For being-in-itself is not active; in order that there may be ends and means there must already be being. And the in-itself is first being before it can be utilized as passive by a human subject.

Furthermore, being-in-itself is also beyond negation and affirmation. Since affirmation is always affirmation *of* something, then the affirmative act is distinguished from the thing affirmed. But if we have an affirmation in which the affirmed totally coincides with the affirming act, then this affirmation cannot be affirmed, because the known is *in* the knower without any duality. This, says Sartre is how being exists. It is like the known in the knower; it relates to itself without any duality. Could we say then that such being-in-itself is total immanence? Even this is somewhat misleading, since immanence implies the slightest possible distance of self from self. But being-in-itself is purely self. We must think of it as an immanence that cannot realize itself, an affirmation that cannot affirm itself, an activity that cannot act, because it totally coincides with itself. In other words, being is simply in-itself. Sartre gives his best description of it in one line: "Uncreated, without reason for being, without any connection with another being, being-in-itself is *de trop* for eternity."[22]

Being for-itself

As is clear from the above analysis intuition has revealed to us simultaneously both the in-itself and the for-itself; the former is the transphenomenal being of phenomena, and the latter is the transphenomenal being of human consciousness.

We have described being-in-itself above as being so self-indentical that it admits not the slightest of interstices; it is so crammed full of itself that it cannot even affirm itself. Against this definition of in-itself we can understand that of for-itself. The for-itself is precisely this same in-itself now trying to become a being which can affirm itself. For-itself is the rupture in this whole of in-itself. Consciousness implies consciousness of self; as such therefore, it means duality, a reflected and a reflecting. This is being-for-itself. If in-itself is perfect unity, for-itself is unity affirming itself, and in this very affirmation introducing a fissure into the unity.

[22] *BN*, p. lxvi. "Incréé, sans raison d'être, sans aucun rapport avec un autre être, l'être en soi est *de trop* pour l'éternité." *EN*, p. 34.

"The for-itself," Sartre explains, "is, in fact, nothing but the pure nihilation of the in-itself; it is like a hole of being at the heart of Being."[23] He adds, however, that the for-itself is not the nihilation of a great complete whole such as the Parmenidean absolute unity. Rather it is the nihilation of the individual in-itself. "It is the nihilation of an individual and particular in-itself, and not of a being in general. The for-itself is not nothingness in general but a particular privation; it constitutes itself as the privation of *this being*."[24]

This nihilation of the in-itself, whereby, so to speak, it stands off at a distance from itself, affirms itself, is conscious being. "To be other than being is to be self-consciousness. . . . For the only way in which the other can exist as other is to be consciousness (of) being other. Otherness is, in fact, an internal negation, and only a consciousness can be constituted as an internal negation."[25]

If the for-itself or conscience being, arises from the nihilation of the in-itself then we may well ask what causes this emergence of the for-itself. Is not the in-itself self-sufficient, independent? It now appears that the in-itself is not so self-sufficient as we were first led to believe. The in-itself is "*sans raison, sans cause et sans nécessité*," but it is not *causa sui*. The emergence of the for-itself represents the attempt of the in-itself to become perfectly self-sufficient and self explanatory. Sartre concludes therefore, that the for-itself seems to arise from the efforts of the in-itself to become its own cause, for the in-itself, though absolute (it cannot be deduced) is still contingent (it could as well not be as be).

At this point the reader sees a contradiction staring him in the face, for the in-itself is apparently acting like a for-itself. And Sartre sees it also. But with a touch of legerdemain he dissolves it. We must distinguish he tells us, between ontology and metaphysics. Ontology only describes; metaphysics seeks causes and origins. Sartre is doing ontology. He can therefore only describe for the metaphysician what does happen. It is then up to the latter to attempt hypotheses that explain why and how it happens. Ontology can, however, provide two key facts that the metaphysician must keep in mind.

[23] *BN*, p. 617. "Le Pour-soi, en effet, n'est pas autre chose que la pure néantisation de l'En-soi, il est comme un trou d'être au sein de l'Etre." *EN*, p. 712.

[24] *BN*, p. 618. "Il est néantisation de l'En-soi individuel et singulier et non d'un être en général. Le pour-soi n'est pas le néant en général mais une privation singulière; il se constitue en privation de *cet être-ci*." *EN*, p. 712.

[25] *BN*, p. 618. "Etre autre que l'être, c'est être conscient (de) soi . . . car la seule façon dont l'autre puisse exister comme autre, c'est d'être conscient (d')être autre. L'altérité est, en effet, négation interne et seule une conscience peut se constituer comme négation interne." *EN*, p. 712.

To begin with, says Sartre, "every process of a foundation of the self is a rupture in the identity-of-being of the in-itself, a withdrawal by being in relation to itself and the appearance of presence-to-self or consciousness. It is only by making itself for-itself that being can aspire to be the cause of itself."[26] The second fact that ontology can supply is that "the for-itself is effectively a perpetual project of founding itself qua being and a perpetual failure of this project."[27] But ontology itself cannot solve the contradiction involved in the fact that in order to initiate a project of founding itself, the in-itself would *already* have to be a for-itself.

We are here, obviously, at the most crucial point in the whole Sartrean ontology. The generation of the for-itself through the attempt of the in-itself to become its *causa sui* has brought us face to face with the most basic problem in the entire system. Unless Sartre can explain how the immobile in-itself, frozen in its perfect unity, generates the for-itself, then his analyses would seem highly suspect. Sartre admits the problem: "Ontology here comes up against a profound contradiction, since it is through the for-itself that the possibility of a foundation comes to the world."[28] Incredible as it may seem, to this absolutely primary question in his ontology, Sartre invokes his self-proclaimed priviledge of phenomenology (mere description) and gives the following answer: "Ontology will therefore limit itself to declaring that *everything takes place as if* the in-itself, in a project to found itself, gave itself the modification of the for-itself."[29]

This tremendous bathos has not gone unchallenged by the Sartrean commentators. For it would seem that it is not the limits of ontology but the logic of the system itself that forces Sartre to admit defeat in the ultimate explanation of the generation of the for-itself. To Sartre's weak effort to escape from the dilemma by his "everything takes place as if," Pere Troisfontaines reacts in astonishment: " 'As if' – What's this? If we adhere to the fundamental definitions [of in-itself and for-itself] then surely we cannot explain things in this fashion. . . . In spite of its logical ingenuity, the system is built on a false foundation, on an in-itself that acts like a for-itself

[26] *BN*, p. 620. ". . . tout processus de fondement de soi est rupture de l'être-identique de l'en-soi, recul de l'être par rapport à lui-même et apparition de la présence à soi ou conscience. C'est seulement en se faisant pour-soi que l'être pourrait aspirer à être cause de soi." *EN*, p. 714.

[27] *BN*, p. 620. ". . . le pour-soi est *effectivement* projet perpétuel de se fonder soi-même en tant qu'être et échec perpétuel de ce projet." *EN*, p. 715.

[28] *BN*, p. 620. "L'ontologie se heurte ici à une contradiction profonde, piusque c'est par le pour-soi que la possibilité d'un fondement vient au monde." *EN*, p. 715.

[29] *BN*, p. 621. "L'ontologie se bornera donc à déclarer que *tout se passe comme si* l'en-soi, dans un projet pour se fonder lui-même, se donner la modification du pour-soi." *EN*, p. 715.

– most amazing."[30] And the American commentator, Desan, has similarly expressed shock at Sartre's attempt to derive for-itself from the in-itself. "This is altogether impossible," says Desan, "if the definition of the basic areas of his ontology are to remain true. The being-in-itself, the dumb, massive, brute existent of Sartre's system, cannot plan or intend to become a for-itself. The contradiction is flagrant and the author himelf is obliged to recognize it."[31] But, though recognizing it, Sartre claims as an ontologist that he is not obliged to offer a metaphysical explanation of how the contradiction is to be resolved. And so we are left wondering if this lack of inner consistency in so basic a problem does not undercut the whole Sartrean enterprise. Prescinding from this more ultimate question, however, let us conclude our discussion of the fundamental distinction between the two types of being that Sartre finds in his preliminary analysis by reemphasizing that the in-itself is conceived as pure unity. "Being is what it is . . . the density of being of the in-itself is infinite. It is fullness."[32] The for-itself, by contrast, is necessarily a being that exhibits duality. "The distinguishing characteristic of consciousness, on the other hand, is that it is a decompression of being. Indeed it is impossible to define it as coincidence with itself."[33]

Since the notion of conscious being as a gap constantly trying to fill itself, a need craving satisfaction, is basic for the later description of the person engaged in the eternal, but futile project of attempting to establish himself as a self-sufficient being, an in-itself-for-itself, Sartre describes in great detail the various structures of the for-itself and the ways in which it attempts to fulfill itself. For our purposes it is not necessary to follow him through these lengthy analyses. We shall only note, in concluding our discussion of the for-itself, the identification Sartre makes between the for-itself and freedom. He arrives at this from the basic nihilating power of the for-itself.

We have seen him describe the for-itself as the being that introduces nothingness into the heart of being. This power of negation is essentially freedom. For the for-itself generates nothingness, Sartre tells us, by placing free acts that deny its past and build toward its projected future. "Freedom

[30] "'Comme si,' attention! car à s'en tenir aux définitions cardinales, il n'en peut être *ainsi*. . . . Malgré son ingéniosité logique, le système porte à faux sur un en-soi qui agit – o stupeur! – comme un pour soi." Roger Troisfontaines, *Le Choix de J.-P. Sartre,* 2nd ed., Paris, Aubier, 1949, p. 39.

[31] Wilfred Desan, *The Tragic Finale,* p. 181.

[32] *BN,* p. 74. "L'être est ce qu'il est . . . la densité d'être de l'en-soi est infinie. C'est le plein." *EN,* p. 116.

[33] *BN,* p. 74. "La charactéristique de la conscience, au contraire, c'est qu'elle est une décompression d'être. Il est impossible en effet de la définir comme coïncidence avec soi." *EN,* p. 116.

is the human being putting his past out of play by secreting his own nothingness."[34] Thus, after a long analysis of freedom, Sartre identifies freedom as identical with the being of the for-itself:

> We have shown that freedom is actually one with the being of the for-itself; human reality is free to the exact extent that it has to be its own nothingness. It has to be this nothingness, as we have seen, in multiple dimensions: first, by temporalizing itself – i.e. by being always at a distance from itself, which means that it can never let itself be determined by its past to perform this or that particular act; second, by rising up as a consciousness of something and (of) itself – i.e., by being presence to itself and not simply self, which implies that nothing exists in consciousness which is not consciousness of existing and that consequently nothing external to consciousness can motivate it; and finally, by being transcendence – i.e. not something which would *first* be in order subsequently to put itself into relation with this or that end, but on the contrary, a being which is originally a project – i.e., which is defined by its end.[35]

Under what form does human freedom reveal itself to consciousness as being the very nature of the human being? "It is in anguish," says Sartre, "that man gets the consciousness of his freedom . . . it is in anguish that freedom is, in its being, in question for itself."[36] And thus Sartre invokes the category – anguish – that has dominated existential thought since the days of Kierkegaard. The for-itself finds itself as the pardoxical gap in being, and in the face of its nothingness, it can only experience the anguish of the unfulfilled.

[34] *BN*, p. 28. "La liberté c'est l'être humain mettant son passé hors de jeu en sécrétant son propre néant." *EN*, p. 65.

[35] *BN*, p. 453. "Nous avons montré que la liberté ne faisait qu'une avec l'être du Pour-soi: la réalité humaine est libre dans une mesure exacte où elle a à être son propre néant. Ce néant nous l'avons vu, elle a à l'être dans de multiples dimensions: d'abord en se temporisant, c'est-à-dire en étant toujours à distance d'elle même, ce qui implique qu'elle ne peut jamais se laisser déterminer par son passé à tel ou tel acte – ensuite en surgissant comme conscience de quelque-chose et (de) soi-même, c'est-à-dire en étant présente à soi et non simplement soi, ce qui implique que rien n'existe dans la conscience qui ne soit conscience d'exister et que, en conséquence, rien d'extérieur à la conscience ne peut la motiver – enfin en étant transcendance, c'est-à-dire non pas quelque chose qui serait *d'abord* pour se mettre *ensuite* en relation avec telle ou telle fin, mais au contraire un être qui est originellement projet, c'est-à-dire qui se définit par sa fin." *EN*, p. 529–530.

[36] *BN*, p. 29. "C'est dans l'angoisse que l'homme prend conscience de sa liberté . . . c'est dans l'angoisse que la liberté est dans son être en question pour elle-même." *EN*, p. 66.

CHAPTER II

THE INTERSUBJECTIVE DIALECTIC

Such is the man of Sartre as a description of the structure of the for-itself reveals him. He is eternally destined to projects that fail. He is a gap in being, an emptiness conscious of its own vacuity, and constantly striving to attain the status of in-itself without losing that of for-itself. This attempt to become an in-itself-for-itself simultaneously is what Sartre calls our basic project. Such a being would be what all men have always called by the name of "God;" i.e., a being who is simultaneously conscious being and yet perfect *causa sui*. "God . . . represents the permanent limit in terms of which man makes known to himself what he is. To be man means to reach toward being God."[1] This fundamental attempt of man to make himself in-itself-for-itself (or God), is destined necessarily to frustration, because by their nature these two types of being are mutually incompatible. By definition, "God" is a contradictory notion.

It is in connection with man's futile attempt to achieve this goal and to heal the dividedness of his being that Sartre raises the question of the "other" subject. The "other" serves a double function in the Sartrean ontology. For it simultaneously reveals a hitherto unrealized structure of the for-itself, which Sartre calls my being-for-others, and it also provides the principal means by which the for-itself strives to solve the unsolvable – to become the in-itself-for-itself. For it seems at first as if the other may serve as the catalyst by which the conscious subject can capture the self-identify of in-itself without losing its own for-itself character.

Sartre's discussion of intersubjectivity therefore involves two major questions: (1) how we arrive at the existence of the other; and (2) what kind of relationships we can establish with another.

[1] *BN*, p. 566. "Dieu . . . représente la limite permanente à partir de laquelle l'homme se fait annoncer ce qu'il est. Etre homme c'est tendre à être Dieu." *EN*, p. 653.

The Existence of the Other Person

From our analyses up to this point, says Sartre, we have discovered that the human being is specifically a being for-itself. By continuing further, however, we encounter modes of consciousness which indicate a type of structure radically different. This additional ontological structure is *my* being without being being-*for-me*. Briefly, this new aspect of my ontological structure is "my-existence-*for-the-other*" as other than himself. It is my being-for-the-other. It is a structure of my being determined by the other, mediated by him. By reflection on this structure we come to see ourselves as the object for the other as subject. With this reflection upon certain specific states of consciousness, we can discover that these are caused by the fact of the other person present to me. The "stare" of the other engenders in me this new ontological structure which was not there before and which could arrive only by the agency of the other. This new being that the other has revealed in me is being-for-the-other. In order therefore to know fully the dimensions of the self we should have to include its relations with the other. These relations are not only of an external nature; they contribute to the very internal structure of the self. By this reflection upon certain states of consciousness, therefore, we shall simultaneously discover the existence of the other person and be able to fill out more completely the outline we have made of the internal structure of the self.

Before setting forth his own "proof" of the existence of the other person, Sartre undertakes a criticism of previous philosophy dealing with this point. It will be valuable here to note briefly wherein he finds the weakness of other solutions. We may then see more clearly why Sartre feels that his own approach is more valid.

1. Deficiences of Realism and Idealism

Realism, he tells us, has been curiously untroubled by the problem of the existence of the other. In the same way that the rest of the exterior world is simply "given," realism appears to believe that the other person also is "given." "In the midst of the real what is more real than the Other?"[2] But despite the fact that realism solves the problem of knowledge in general by the action of the world on the thinking substance, it does not propose immediate and reciprocal action of thinking substances among themselves. Rather, it is by the intermediary of the body that they communicate; between my consciousness and that of the other, both my body and his must

[2] *BN*, p. 223. "Au milieu du réel, en effet, quoi de plus réel qu'autrui?" *EN*, p. 277.

intervene as necessary mediators. "The Other's soul is therefore separated from mine by all the distance which separates first my soul from my body, then my body from the Other's body, and finally the Other's body from his soul."[3]

Now if souls are separated by their bodies, they are totally distinct, and we cannot conceive of any immediate presence of one to the other. Even if we say that the body of the other is present by intuition, this does not help us. "Realism in taking this position and presenting us with a body not enveloped in human totality, but apart, like a stone or a tree or a piece of wax, has killed the body as surely as the physiologist who with his scalpel separates a piece of flesh from the totality of the living being. It is not the *Other's body* which is present to the realist intuition, but *a* body."[4]

In the few instances in which realistic philosophers have made an effort to determine how one person knows the other, Sartre says, they have failed to advance very far. The realistic and positivistic psychology of the nineteenth century took for granted the existence of the other and concerned itself only with the means by which it could decipher the reactions of the other. The hypothesis on which its work rested was the hypothesis of analogy. By comparing my own reactions to those manifested by the other, the psychology of analogy postulated a soul like my own behind the body of the other. Such a theory, however, can only give me a probability that the other person exists, for "it remains always possible that the Other is only a body."[5] On this basis, indeed, we could as well postulate a similar soul in animals and follow behaviorism to the limit.

Another realistic attempt to solve the problem of the other is found in the more modern theories of empathy and sympathy. Even these, however, do not clearly establish the existence of the other as certain, Sartre declares. (We shall have occasion in a later chapter to examine these theories when dealing with Scheler's work.)

Realism, concludes Sartre, cannot solve the problem of the other; it eventually leads us in fact, only to subjective idealism. "If the body is a real object really acting on thinking substance, the Other becomes a pure repre-

[3] *BN,* p. 223. "L'âme d'autrui est donc séparée de la mienne par toute la distance qui sépare tout d'abord mon âme de mon corps, puis mon corps du corps d'autrui, enfin le corps d'autrui de son âme." *EN,* p. 277.

[4] *BN,* p. 223. "La position du réalisme en nous livrant le corps non point enveloppé dans la totalité humaine mais à part, comme une pierre ou un arbre ou un morceau de cire, a tué aussi sûrement le corps que le scalpel du physiologiste en séparant un morceau de chair de la totalité du vivant. Ce n'est pas le *corps d'autrui* qui est présent à l'intuition réaliste: c'est *un* corps." *EN,* p. 278.

[5] *BN,* p. 224. "... il reste toujours probable qu'autrui ne soit qu'un corps." *EN,* p. 278.

sentation, whose *esse* is a simple *percipi;* that is, one whose existence is measured by the knowledge which we have of it." [6]

The haven of idealism, however, can offer scant comfort to us in this problem. Sartre goes to great lengths to prove that in terms of Kantianism the concept of "the other person" cannot be established either as a constitutive or as a regulative concept. In the face of this insufficiency, idealism has only two possible solutions left: either the position of solipsism, or the affirmation of the real existence of the other. But the first of these ways is untenable, for there is no justification for denying the existence of the other; and the second position is a return to realism which we have just left.

Now the fundamental reason for Sartre why realism and idealism fail to advance very far in their attempt to solve the problem of the other is because they begin from a basic presupposition which is false. They see correctly that the other is the one who is "not me;" but they both make this negation a negation of *exteriority*. "This *not* indicates a nothingness as a *given* element of separation between the Other and myself." [7] There is thus posed between persons a spatial relation which separates rather than unites them. For both idealism and realism, therefore, since the other is revealed to me in a spatial world, there is a real or an ideal space which separates me from the other. Consequently we are forced either to bridge this gap by invoking God, or to fall back on probable certitude and ultimately solipsism. Even in using God, however, the problem comes back upon us, for He is the quintessence of the "other person," and hence would have to be already in a relation of interiority with me.

We cannot, therefore, begin by posing the other as separated from me by a negation of exteriority. Sartre adumbrates his own solution:

> It seems therefore that a positive theory of the Other's existence must be able simultaneously to avoid solipsism and to dispense with a recourse to God if it envisages my original relation to the Other as an internal negation; that is, as a negation which posits the original distinction between the Other and myself as being such that it determines me by means of the Other and determines the Other by means of me.[8]

[6] *BN*, p. 224. "Si le corps est un objet réel agissant réellement sur la substance pensante, autrui devient une pure représentation, dont l'*esse* est un simple *percipi*, c'est-à-dire dont l'existence est mesurée par la connaissance que nous en avons." *EN*, p. 279.

[7] *BN*, p. 230. "Ce *ne-pas* indique un néant comme élément de séparation *donné* entre autrui et moi-même." *EN*, p. 285.

[8] *BN*, p. 232. "Il semble donc qu'une théorie positive de l'existence d'autrui devrait pouvoir à la fois éviter la solipsisme et se passer du recours à Dieu si elle envisage ma relation originelle à autrui comme une négation d'intériorité, c'est-à-dire comme

2. Deficiencies of Husserl, Hegel and Heidegger

Sartre mentions three modern philosophers who have been partially right in their approach to the problem of the other person, but who fail to push far enough to render a complete solution. Husserl, negating the intersubstantial solution, proposed an inter-monadic one, wherein each object was constituted by a series of references. He tried correctly to show that I am what I am essentially in relation to another person. But unfortunately he proposed a relation that was both external and resting on a cognitive basis, and so failed to penetrate to the heart of the problem. Hegel went further, Sartre believes, because he saw that the relation between two persons must be internal. (The description of master and slave in Hegel's *Phenomenology of Spirit* unquestionably had great influence on Sartre's own solution wherein one consciousness attempts to absorb the other, constituting itself by the reduction of the other.) But Hegel, though making the relation internal, still preserved it on the plane of *knowledge* of one self by the other. With the analysis of Heidegger we come finally to see the problem posed correctly. He has seen that if we are to avoid solipsism we must establish the relationship of the self to the other as a relationship of *being* and not of knowledge. Sartre praises Heidegger for the direction of his solution: "At least his theory fulfills these two requirements: (1) the relation between 'human-realities' must be a relation of being; (2) this relation must cause 'human-realities' to depend on one another in their essential being." [9]

Once we have put the question of the knowledge of the other in these terms, the problem disappears, for the other is now no longer a particular existence which I encounter, rather: "He is the ex-centric limit which contributes to the constitution of my being." [10] With all previous philosophy, the relation between selves was of the "being-for" type; with Heidegger the other is no longer object "for" me, but "with" me, for each person is essentially a "*Mitsein*," a "being-with," existing in a reciprocal lateral interdependence with each other "*Mitsein.*"

Although Sartre honors Heidegger for his solution, he avers that he failed to establish one crucial point: he does not establish how *this* concrete man

une négation qui pose la distinction originelle d'autrui et de moi-même dans la mesure exacte où elle me détermine par autrui et où elle détermine autrui par moi." *EN*, p. 288.

[9] *BN*, p. 244. "Au moins sa théorie répond-elle à ces deux exigences. 1° la relation des 'réalités-humaines" doit être une relation d'être; 2° cette relation doit faire dépendre les 'réalités humaines' les unes des autres en leur être essentiel." *EN*, p. 301.

[10] *BN*, p. 245. "C'est le terme ex-centrique qui contribue à la constitution de mon être." *EN*, p. 301.

contacts *that* man. The theory of "existing-together" is impeccable in the abstract, but it sins against the individual man.

3. *The Conditions for a Solution*

Such, then, have been the attempts made by previous philosophers to solve the problem of the existence of the other person. With a sweeping condemnation of these attempts as insufficient, a gesture reminiscent of Kant's condemnation of all previous metaphysics before launching forth on the critical philosophy, Sartre declares that he will now lay down the necessary and sufficient conditions under which alone a theory of the existence of the other person will be valid. Where Kant laid down the universal conditions for the possibility of any knowledge at all, Sartre will lay down the conditions for the possibility of the existence of the other person and of our relations with him. Having set these conditions he will then present his own theory as the only one which can fulfill them.

What are these conditions? Sartre mentions only four. We shall note them briefly and then pass on to examine the Sartrean theory which he claims will satisfy all conditions.

1) There can be no question of a strict "proof" of the existence of the other. His existence must be as certain as my own, otherwise all speculation on it is useless. A theory of the existence of the other therefore, ought simply to clarify and precise the meaning of my affirmation of his existence, and far from inventing a proof, ought to make explicit the foundation of this certitude. Just as Descartes did not prove his existence, because he had always known it, so I have always known that the other existed by a "comprehension preontologique." Therefore, there must be something resembling the *Cogito* which we must use to validate the affirmation of the other.

2) The failure of Hegel to reach the other in his existence has shown us that the only possible starting point for us is the cartesian *Cogito.* The *Cogito,* therefore, upon reexamination, will bear me outward to the other exactly as it has to the in-itself, "not by revealing to me an a priori structure of myself which would point toward an equally a priori Other, but by disclosing to me the concrete, indubitable presence of a particular, concrete Other, just as it has already revealed to me my own incomparable, contingent but necessary, and concrete existence." [11]

It is thus the for-itself itself which will lead us beyond the for-itself, im-

[11] *BN,* p. 251. "non pas en me révélant une structure *a priori* de moi-même qui pointerait vers un autrui également *a priori* mais en me découvrant la présence concrète et indubitable de *tel* ou *tel* autrui concret, comme il m'a déjà révélé mon existence incomparable, contingente, nécessaire pourtant, et concrète." *EN,* p. 308.

manence which will yield transcendence: "In my own inmost depths I must find not *reasons for believing* that the Other exists but the Other himself as not being me." [12]

3) What the *Cogito* reveals to us cannot be the other as "object." If the other is only object of my knowledge, his existence can never be more than probable, as is that of all objects.

4) Finally, the *Cogito* ought to reveal the other to me as that which is not me. Such a negation can take two forms. It may be a negation of pure externality, separating one being from another. This would not suffice here, for in such a case, all knowledge of the other, says Sartre, would be by definition impossible. What is required is internal negation, a dialectical reciprocity by which each of the two terms constitutes itself by denying that it is the other.

Sartre's Theory

The chapter of his book in which Sartre's sets forth his own theory of the existence of the other is entitled "The Look." Although at first sight this might seem an affectation of the dramatic in an ontological inquiry, a careful reading of the lengthy chapter reveals that in reality it is the most apt word to describe the whole thesis of Sartre. Reduced to its simplest form, the thesis says that the existence of the other person is revealed to me immediately and absolutely by the fact of my being-for-the-other. When do I experience myself as "existing for the other"? When he looks at me, says Sartre. "The look" is the key to the existence of the other.

To elucidate his theory Sartre analyzes a concrete encounter with the other person. Let us suppose, says Sartre, that I am in a public park. Around me stretches a green lawn and on the lawn are benches. Nearby a man is walking along. I see this man and know him as another object like the benches; but I also know him as more than object. What does it mean to say that I affirm of this object that it is a man? Certainly we see that it makes some difference, for if I viewed him only as another object, as a puppet perhaps, I would apply to him the categories which normally suffice to group spatio-temporal objects. I would include him among the other objects in my view by a purely "additif" relation with them. "In short, no new relation would appear *through him* between those things in my universe: grouped and synthesized *from my point of view* into instrumental com-

[12] *BN*, p. 251. "au plus profond de moi-même je dois trouver non *des raisons de croire* à autrui, mais autrui lui-même comme n'étant pas moi." *EN*, p. 309.

plexes, they would *from his* disintegrate into multiplicities of indifferent relations."[13]

But since I perceive him *as a man,* this whole relationship changes. I see him as a center about which the other objects of my world begin to be grouped. Whereas before his entrance, the objects of the world were oriented toward me, now there is danger that they will escape from me to him. The relations of external negation and distance which I have set up among the objects of my world now threaten to disintegrate into non-spatial relations centering on him by the very fact that he sees them. Thus, the first warning signal I have that another person has entered my world is this realization of the possibility of a disintegration of my objective universe, of a "draining away" of my world toward him. The other person first appears, therefore, as a negation of me, as an infringement of the world that I have ordered about me. The other first appears as the one who can constitute his own world by dissolving mine. The other is the enemy who menaces my world. "Thus suddenly an object has appeared which has stolen the world from me . . . . The appearance of the Other in the world corresponds therefore to a fixed sliding of the whole universe, to a decentralization of the world which undermines the centralization which I am simultaneously effecting."[14]

Up to this point of the analysis, we have been considering the other person still as "object." He has not yet turned his face to me; he is still an object in "my" world, albeit an object who threatens to rob me of my world. How then do I come to perceive him as subject? It must be, says Sartre, from the possibility that he can include me in his world an another object. "It is in and through the revelation of my being-as-object for the Other that I must be able to apprehend the presence of his being-as-subject."[15]

In a word, the existence of the other as subject is given as certain because I find myself existing as an "object." If the other were only object he could not thus reduce me from my status as free subjectivity; therefore the other exists as subject. Within the depths of the self, thus, we find the other subject: i.e., the structure of the self as being-for-the-other reveals the existence of the other as subject who can only manifest his subjectivity to me by

[13] *BN,* p. 254. "En un mot, aucune relation neuve n'apparaîtrait par lui entre ces choses de mon univers: groupées et synthétisées *de mon côté* en complexes instrumentaux, elles se désagrégeraient *du sien* en multiplicités de relations d'indifférence." *EN,* p. 311.

[14] *BN,* p. 255. "Ainsi tout à coup un objet est apparu qui m'a volé le monde. . . . l'apparition d'autrui dans le monde, correspond donc à un glissement figé de tout l'univers, à une décentralition du monde qui mine par en dessous la centralisation que j'opère dans le même temps." *EN,* p. 313.

[15] *BN,* p. 256. "C'est dans et par la révélation de mon être-objet pour autrui que je dois pouvoir saisir la présence de son être-sujet." *EN,* p. 314.

reducing me to the "object" status. When do I experience myself existing as object for the other? Actually I experience this whenever another looks at me. When the man in the park turns and includes me in his view, I experience myself *being known* along with the lawn, the trees and the benches as an object for the other. In certain states of consciousness, however, this experience is more striking, and clearly reveals the agency of the other in the constitution of the for-itself. Such is the experience of shame. Sartre illustrates it succinctly: "I have just made an awkward or vulgar gesture. This gesture clings to me; I neither judge it nor blame it. I simply live it. I realize it in the mode of for-itself. But now suddenly I raise my head. Somebody was there and has seen me. Suddenly I realize the vulgarity of my gesture, and I am ashamed."[16]

In no way is this shame a mere product of reflexive consciousness; rather the presence of the other provokes it: "the Other is the indispensable mediator between myself and me; I am ashamed of myself as *I appear* to the Other."[17] A simple examination discloses that "vulgarity" implies a relation to another. "Nobody can be vulgar all alone."[18] The other, therefore, has not only revealed to me what I am, rather he has constituted me a new type of being. Before the appearance of the other I was not this being and without his mediation I could not have become it, because this new type of being that I am is precisely my being-for-the-other. "This new being which appears *for* the Other does not reside *in* the Other . . . . Thus shame is shame *of oneself before the Other.*"[19]

The other's looking upon me has changed the whole situation. Before this, I as subject organized the world about myself, and included the other among the objects of my immediate universe. Now, with the look of the other fastened on me, my whole world crumbles away; instead of being the center of my universe, I am reduced to an object in the world of the other-subject. This required a radical change in the status of the other. This new status in which the other-object is transformed into other-subject simultaneously reduces me from the status of a subject to that of an object in the world of the other. The active principle which effects this reduction of my

[16] *BN,* p. 221. "Je viens de faire un geste maladroit ou vulgaire: ce geste colle à moi, je ne le juge ni le blâme, je le vis simplement, je le réalise sur le mode du pour-soi. Mais voici tout à coup que je lève la tête: quelqu'un était là et m'a vu. Je réalise tout à coup toute la vulgarité de mon geste et j'ai honte." *EN,* p. 276.

[17] *BN,* p. 222. ". . . autrui est le médiateur indispensable entre moi et moi-même: j'ai honte de moi *tel que j'apparaîs* à autrui." *EN,* p. 276.

[18] *BN,* p. 222. "On n'est pas vulgaire tout seul." *EN,* p. 276.

[19] *BN,* p. 222. "Cet être nouveau qui apparaît *pour* autrui ne réside pas *en* autrui; . . . ainsi la honte est honte *de soi devant autrui.*" *EN,* p. 276.

ontological status is the *look of the other*. The corresponding state engendered in me whereby I become aware of my reduction, or, what is the same, whereby I become aware of the other person existing as subject, is the "being-seen-by-the-other."

This "being-seen-by-the-other" represents a totally new state, one that cannot be deduced either from the essence of other-object, or from my being-as-subject. The other-object represented the permanent possibility of the disintegration of my world; he is revealed to me as subject when this possibility begins to come into actuality. "He is that object in the world which determines an internal flow of the universe, an internal hemorrhage. He is the subject who is revealed to me in that flight of myself toward objectivation."[20]

To the initial inquiry about the existence of the other person, Sartre has given this ingenious answer: I am aware of the other person because I find myself reduced from subject to object. A new dimension of the self, the "being-seen-by-the-other" simultaneously reduces me to object in the world of the other, and also yields me the existence of the other-subject.

We see now why Sartre has entitled his "proof" of the existence of the other "the look." By analysis, he has come upon a state of consciousness in which I feel myself existing, no longer as for-myself, as a subjectivity ordering the universe in concentric fashion about myself, but rather as being-for-the-other. I am conscious of existing for another person, and of existing as an "object" for him. Now I can exist as an object only for someone who is himself "subject." Therefore, in the experience of myself as object for another, I come to discover him as subject. My consciousness of "being seen" by the other has been the starting point for the discovery of the other as subject. Such, in brief, is the Sartrean method of arriving at the existence of the other. It does not postulate "knowledge" of the other in the sense of looking out from my subjectivity toward another being whom I invest with subjectivity. On the contrary, within the very structure of my own being I find the other as modification of my being. Just as I exist for-myself so also do I exist for-the-other. These two types of existence are not contrary; they are two facets of my structure as conscious being.

We may note also the fact that the mode of discovery of the other dictates the kind of relations which I may have with him. The stare of the other is an attack on my subjectivity, an invasion of my world, a reduction of me to an object in the world of the starer, a transcending of my own transcendence.

[20] *BN,* p. 257. "Il est cet objet du monde qui détermine un écoulement interne de l'univers, une hémorragie interne; il est le sujet qui se découvre à moi dans cette fuite de moi-même vers l'objectivité." *EN,* p. 315.

The other first appears, therefore, as one who is opposed to me. This is the basic position which two selves take toward one another. The various relations between persons which Sartre describes are all particular instances of this fundamental relation of opposition and conflict. There are, in his view, no other types of relations possible between human beings. "Conflict is the original meaning of being-for-others."[21]

The Relations with Other Persons

The for-itself is constantly engaged, as we have said previously, in a fundamental and eternally futile project to found itself, to become simultaneously an in-itself-for-itself. With the appearance of the other person in consciousness, says Sartre, there occurs the most important opportunity for the for-itself to achieve fullness of being.

We have explained above the power which the stare of the other has to alienate me into an object *for him,* to reveal me as being-for-the-other. Now this in a sense is a reduction of me to an in-itself. The other sees me not as a for-itself and subjectivity, but as an object like the rest of objects, an in-itself. The features of the for-itself are thus reduced by his objectifying stare into those of an in-itself. Does not this act of the other, therefore, accomplish my project of reaching the state of an in-itself? Unfortunately, no. True, the other reduces me to an in-itself, but in this case I become an in-itself not for myself, but only for him. I do not provide the foundation for this in-itself character which comes to me, but *he does.*

The power of the other to reduce me to an in-itself, however, has at least shown the way which may be taken. If I can somehow lay hold of this agent who effects my reduction to an in-itself, if I can somehow "absorb" the other who possesses this power of objectifying me, then I will have reached the goal of becoming an in-itself-for-itself.

All my relations with the other person, therefore, will be motivated by a single aim: to possess this other freedom which has power of making me object. It should be said at the outset that I cannot succeed. For what I want to possess is the free subjectivity of the other. But by the very nature of things I can never do so. For if I attempt to seize his freedom, the assertion of my subjectivity reduces him to freedom-less object; and if I make myself object to entrap his freedom, my own freedom reasserts itself. Either approach results in frustration. When one fails I try the other; the process is endless and success is impossible.

[21] *BN,* p. 364. "Le conflit est le sens originel de l'être-pour-autrui." *EN,* p. 431.

The first attitude toward the other is an attempt to trap the freedom of the other completely in myself seen as object. It proceeds through three steps: love, language, masochism.

Love, says Sartre, is the desire to be loved. It is the attempt of the self, made object by the other, to conquer and possess that center of freedom which has power of sustaining the self as object. Sartre has some remarkable and powerful arguments to back up his view. The following two paragraphs are only a sampling:

> For if in one sense my being-as-object is an unbearable contingency and the pure "possession" of myself by another, still in another sense this being stands as the indication of what I should be obliged to recover and found in order to be the foundation of myself. But this is conceivable only if I assimilate the Other's freedom. Thus my project of recovering myself is fundamentally a project of absorbing the Other.[22]
>
> Whereas before being loved we were uneasy about that unjustified, unjustifiable protuberance which was our existence, whereas we felt ourselves *"de trop,"* we now feel that our existence is taken up and willed even in its tiniest details by an absolute freedom which at the same time our existence conditions and which we ourselves will with our freedom. This is the basis for the joy of love when there is joy: we feel that our existence is justified.[23]

Thus it is clear that for Sartre the role of the loved one is simply that of a useful object. No importance is attached to him except insofar as he can offer me the opportunity of establishing myself amid the welter of nothingness that I feel myself to be. The other appears as the being that offers me the opportunity to overcome my ontological insufficiency. If only I can "absorb" him, this being who makes me to be object, then perhaps I can reach the goal of becoming an in-itself-for-itself.

The other, however, will not willingly submit to being absorbed by me, for in so doing, his own transcendence is lost and his freedom frozen. In this case, therefore, the self has only one path open to it: It must seduce the other. For Sartre, love means nothing else. In seduction, says Sartre, I do

[22] *BN*, p. 364. "Car, si, en un sens, mon être-objet est contingence insupportable et pure 'possession' de moi par un autre, en un autre sens cet être est comme l'indication de ce qu'il faudrait que je récupère et que je fonde pour être fondement de moi. Mais c'est ce qui n'est concevable que si je m'assimile la liberté d'autrui. Ainsi, mon projet de récupération de moi est fondamentalement projet de résorption de l'autre." *EN*, p. 432.

[23] *BN*, p. 371. "Au lieu que, avant d'être aimés, nous étions inquiets de cette protubérance injustifiée, injustifiable qu'était notre existence; au lieu de nous sentir 'de trop.' nous sentons à présent que cette existence est reprise et voulue dans ses moindres détails par une liberté absolue qu'elle conditionne en même temps – et que nous voulons nous-mêmes avec notre propre liberté. C'est là le fond de la joie d'amour, lorsqu'elle existe: nous sentir justifiés d'exister." *EN*, p. 439.

not reveal my subjectivity to the other; rather, I accept my state of objectivity which the "look" of the other has engendered and I seek to engage the total freedom of the other in myself as object by making myself "objet fascinant." I do this by "language," not in the restricted sense of verbal expression, but in the more basic and primitive sense of expressiveness in general, or "mon corps pour l'autre."

Love, however, in its very nature is essentially self-frustrating. For, if by seduction, the self should be able to engender love in the other, note what thereby happens: "Each of the lovers is entirely the captive of the Other inasmuch as each wishes to make himself loved by the Other to the exclusion of anyone else; but at the same time each one demands from the other a love which is not reducible to the 'project of being loved.'"[24] There is no solution here; by engendering love in the other, the self defeats its own project.

Faced with such frustration on the plane of love, the self makes another effort to engulf the subjectivity of the other. It attempts to reduce itself to nothing but an object, so completely that it appears even to itself as object before the other's total freedom. This says Sartre is masochism, which is "a perpetual effort to *annihilate* the subject's subjectivity by causing it to be assimilated by the Other; this effort is accompanied by the exhausting and delicious consciousness of failure so that finally it is the failure itself which the subject ultimately seeks as his principal goal."[25] Thus, masochism, like love, is self-defeating. For by its very nature it leads the subject to a renewed concentration on itself – a revived consciousness of its non-object character – rather than to the success of its project of ensnaring the other.

When these three attempts to entrap the subjectivity of the other by my object-character lead to failure, as they always must, then I turn, says Sartre, to the second basic approach – I try to seize the other's freedom, to transcend his transcendence. This approach has four variations: indifference, desire, hate, and sadism.

In indifference, I attempt to shore up my own subjectivity by the collapse of the freedom of the other. I treat others whom I meet solely as depersonalized functionaries – as the ticket collector at the theatre or the waiter in a

[24] *BN*, p. 375. "Chacun des amants est entièrement captif de l'autre en tant qu'il veut se faire aimer par lui à l'exclusion de tout autre; mais en même temps, chacun exige de l'autre un amour qui ne se réduit nullement au 'projet d'être-aimé.'" *EN*, p.443.

[25] *BN*, p. 379. "... un perpétuel effort pour anéantir la subjectivité du sujet en la faisant réassimiler par l'autre et que cet effort est accompagné de l'épuisante et délicieuse conscience de l'échec, au point que c'est l'échec lui-même que le sujet finit par rechercher comme son but principal." *EN*, p. 447.

restaurant – and thus attempt to make their freedom something at my disposal. Here, too, success eludes me. For with the assertion of myself as subject, the freedom of the other retreats beyond my grasp and leaves me with the other-object.

The attempt to possess the freedom of the other may take the form of sexual desire. Desire, says Sartre, is the endeavor to trap the free subjectivity of the other person in the bonds of his own fleshly existence. But this effort too, is a self-defeating one; in order to produce the incarnation of the other, I must first myself become flesh, and thus I trap myself as well and the project is lost sight of.

The third form in which one person may try to seize the freedom of the other is sadism. Sadism is an attempt to incarnate the other by force and violence. It is the freedom of the other that the sadist tries to seize, but that freedom always escapes him, for the look of the other is powerful enough to destroy any success the sadist may seem to be achieving. For "this explosion of the Other's look in the world of the sadist causes the meaning and goal of sadism to collapse. The sadist discovers that it was *that freedom* which he wished to enslave, and at the same time he realizes the futility of his efforts."[26]

The last effort the self can make to possess the subjectivity of the other is hate. This too is ineffectual. Even if one should go to the limit of murdering the other, this does not undo the fact that the other has existed and the self has been object for him. This encroachment on my being cannot be effaced. "Hate simply represents the final attempt, the attempt of despair," says Sartre. "After the failure of this attempt nothing remains for the for-itself except to re-enter the circle and allow itself to be indefinitely tossed from one to the other of the two fundamental attitudes."[27]

There is, therefore, no solution, no escape from this conflict of self with the other in which neither can win, but in which both must continue in ceaseless conflict. "It is therefore useless for human-reality to seek to get out of this dilemma; one must either transcend the Other or allow oneself to be transcended by him. The essence of the relations between consciousnesses is not the *Mitsein:* it is conflict."[28]

[26] *BN,* p. 406. "... cette explosion du regard d'Autrui dans le monde du sadique fait s'effondrer le sens et le but du sadisme. En même temps le sadisme découvre que c'était *cette liberté-là* qu'il voulait asservir et, en même temps, il se rend compte de la vanité de ses efforts." *EN,* p. 477.

[27] *BN,* p. 412. "La haîne représente simplement l'ultime tentative, la tentative du désespoir. Après l'échec de cette tentative, il ne reste plus au pour-soi qu'à rentrer dans le cercle et à se laisser indéfiniment ballotter de l'une à l'autre des deux attitudes fondamentales." *EN,* p. 484.

[28] *BN,* p. 429. "C'est en vain que la réalité humaine chercherait à sortir de ce

Now Sartre is well aware that the dismal picture he has presented, excluding any subject-to-subject relationships, may cause the reader to object immediately. Are there not, one may ask, situations in which I clearly find myself acting together with another subject – situations in which both of us, as subjects, are engaged in a common enterprise?

Quite true, says Sartre, and in fact, this very experience proves his point. He does not intend to deny that there is such a thing as a "we" experience, in which subjects feel themselves united in interest or action toward a common goal. But he feels that two points must be made: First, the we-experience *presupposes* that each subjectivity has already come to know the other subject by himself experiencing his own "being-as-object-for-the-other." So we do not discover the other subject in the we-experience. Secondly, when subjects find themselves united in a common enterprise, this is not a one-to-one intersubjective relationship directed at the other's subjectivity. Rather it is simply the fact that they are directing themselves to a common goal that unites them in a purely *external* way.

Furthermore, a closer analysis of the we-experience reveals, according to Sartre, the same dialectical structure that we find in the one-to-one situation: When we-as-subjects encounter the other, be he an individual or a group, he is the one who impedes our common aim, and he is thus objectified. Similarly, when we as a group act in resistance to a common project of another we-group, it is clear that they are attempting a reduction of our group to an object status, and we must attempt to do the same to them. Therefore the same basic pattern that we discover in one-to-one relationships dominates all human intercourse, personal as well as social.

Sartre identifies the basic human attitude toward others as one of conflict. This is the simple fact that provides the basis for Sartre's extended analyses presented his latest book, the lengthy *Critique of Dialectical Reason.*

This theme of conflict provides the link between Sartre's ontology and Marxian dialectic. In *Being and Nothingness* the for-itself was identified as a gap seeking closure, a openness seeking filling. For Marx, and for Sartre in his social analysis, man, like all other living things in nature, is a hungry being who must constantly strive to fill his needs. As Desan has pointed out, Sartre's earlier ontological work "showed strikingly that the depth of the nought in man desperately wanted *to be* and that the desire for being brought a permanent attraction toward all that which is *En-soi.* It is toward this plenum that man is incessantly carried."[29]

dilemme: transcender l'autre ou se laisser transcender par lui. L'essence des rapports entre consciences n'est pas le *Mitsein,* c'est le conflit." *EN,* p. 502.

[29] Wilfred Desan, *The Marxism of Jean-Paul Sartre,* N. Y. Doubleday (Anchor), 1966, p. 25.

In his latest book, Sartre simply extends this analysis from one-to-one relationships to social and group relationships. But since conflict is the basic mode of both personal and group relationships, the new book shows us the same theme as the earlier one, but now "writ large," in the clash of the oppressed against their oppressors. Each group constitutes itself as a we-subject to reduce the other group to object status. We have now, not personal, but social dialectic and conflict.

This brief mention of Sartre's modified Marxism in *The Critique of Dialectical Reason* is intended only to point out the social and practical consequences he sees following from the phenomenological analyses of intersubjectivity in *Being and Nothingness.* We do not intend to explore in detail the complex modes of unification by which he finds social groups gradually coming to form in the face of opposition. We shall only point out that there is a grim consistency between the basically Hobbesian view of man from which Sartre started and the Hobbesian view of society to which he comes. For at the very end of his lengthy analysis of man as the for-itself engaged in the futile project of seeking to fill his ontological emptiness, Sartre had succinctly stated the view of man that was to dominate his later social writings:

> Every human reality is a passion in that it projects losing itself so as to found being and by the same stroke to constitute the in-itself which escapes contingency by being its own foundation, the *Ens causa sui,* which religions call God. Thus the passion of man is the reverse of that of Christ, for man loses himself as man in order that God may be born. But the idea of God is contradictory and we lose ourselves in vain. Man is a useless passion.[30]

Such is the final word of Sartre on the possibility of personal community between human beings. Starting from his concept of the person as being-for-itself seeking to establish itself by absorption back into the being-in-itself, he has ended by setting forth his thesis of the eternal frustration of man's efforts at community. Orestes, in Sartre's play dealing with the Greek legend, says to his people before leaving them: "I wish to be a king without a coun-

[30] *BN,* 615. "Chaque réalité humaine est à la fois projet direct de métamorphoser son propre Pour-soi en En-soi-Pour-soi et projet d'appropriation du monde comme totalité d'être-en-soi, sous les espèces d'une qualité fondamentale. Toute réalité humaine est une passion, en ce qu'elle projette de se perdre pour fonder l'être et pour constituer du même coup l'En-soi qui échappe à la contingence en étant son propre fondement, l'*Ens causa sui* qui les religions nomment Dieu. Ainsi la passion de l'homme est-elle inverse de celle du Christ, car l'homme se perd en tant qu'homme pour que Dieu naisse. Mais l'idée de Dieu est contradictoire et nous nous perdons en vain; l'homme est une passion inutile." *EN,* p. 708.

try and without subjects."[31] The line epitomizes the ideal Sartrean man, alone, free, choosing to make his future. This self-constituted isolation is the keynote of his philosophy. Pere Troisfontaines has acutely observed that Sartre's unusual habit of composing his books while sitting in a cafe is in perfect harmony with his outlook.[32] The world of the "*on*," of the stranger, of the casual acquaintance, a world lacking all the normal warmth and intimacy of the home, is the exact counterpart of the world of the in-itself which Sartre has described in his ontological treatises. "L'homme au cafe" is the everyday instance of what in his ontology he has described as the for-itself.

Sartre's philosophy has been called a philosophy of freedom. It could more accurately be described as a philosophy of "aloneness." For Sartrean existentialism is not only a declaration that man is free psychologically. Rather, it proclaims that man is free in the sense that he is isolated in the universe, completely independent of anything other than himself. It is essentially a philosophy of isolation. It cuts away from the person all bonds of whatever kind. Since it presupposes the impossibility of God, it encloses man in the immanence of the temporal sphere; since it further denies man even the possibility of any true community with other men, it leaves each one completely abandoned to himself. Each person, alone and unassisted by any other person above him or beside him is condemned to live out his life in the midst of a world which has no meaning beyond offering possibilities for arbitrary freedom.

For the Sartrean man can be subject only for himself; he is a subjectivity frozen into immobility. Each person can but stare, sphinx-like, out upon other men, knowing them only as he knows the rest of the irrational world. Although they are free subjects like himself, he can never meet them on the plane of subjectivity; he grasps others only as objects.

Like the other objects of the world, other persons are there to be used. Their only value is a use-value. Unlike the other objects of the world, however, other persons are not neutral with respect to the self; rather, they are to be feared and fought, for they threaten to invade the ontological security of the self and rob it of its status as subject.

Hence, the only possible relationship one can have with other persons is that of conflict. Each man, alone and unaided, is condemned to make his own way through a world of "object-persons" which threaten at any moment to fall upon him like brigands and rob him of his one possession, his

[31] "Je veux être un roi sans terre et sans sujets." J.-P. Sartre, *Les Mouches*, Paris, Gallimard, 1943, p. 144.

[32] Troisfontaines, *op. cit.*, p. 55.

free subjectivity. In such a universe, man's only defense is to attack; he can remain free subject only so long as he keeps other persons objects; he must be ever vigilant to paralyze other subjects into objects before they can accomplish this reduction in himself.[33]

The Sartrean man shut up in himself is the very antithesis of the traditional Judeo-Christian man. Not only is he denied any transcendence vertically toward an absolute but he cannot even reach beyond himself to unite with other persons through love. Ontologically he is but a gap in the great unity of being engaged in a futile attempt to fill this vacuity that is himself. He is the power of free choice creating his own essence in the face of an irrational world.

Sartre has proposed, as we have seen, a completely elaborated philosophy aimed at the negation of community. His statement would seem to represent the limit to which such a position may proceed. Despite his efforts to overcome the spectre of solipsism, he has not succeeded. In the dialectic of the in-itself-for-itself there is room for no one but self. It may be that Sartre's philosophy is a faithful reflection of the attitude of the modern man, disillusioned, selfish, engaged only in self-aggrandizement. There are other philosophers, however, who interpret the case differently and who propose a philosophy of community as extremely positive as Sartre's is negative. In the next section we shall examine the theory of a modern philosopher who has opted for community over against isolation.

[33] Desan finds that Sartre's overemphasis on the subjective makes it impossible for him to allow for any intersubjective: "Although Sartre would for all this vehemently reject all accusations of idealism, it should nevertheless be stressed that *no* interpersonal status is present nor accepted *beyond that which proceeds from the subject,* whether from A or in the reverse from B. Some may see the 'intersubjective' in this, but I would be inclined to think that there is much 'subjective' but little 'inter.'" Desan, *Marxism,* p. 272.

SECTION TWO

MAX SCHELER
THE PHENOMENOLOGY OF LIFE

CHAPTER III

SCHELER'S CONCEPT OF *PERSON*

The theory of Sartre on the nature of the human person and his interpersonal relationships which we have outlined in the first section is representative of that branch of existential phenomenology which would deny the possibility of any true community of subjects-as-subjects with one another. The widespread interest in such a view is reflected in the work of other contemporary philosophers and is evident also in the current literature of Europe and America. The gospel of the completely free and independent individual engaged only in his own "project" of "making himself" by his arbitrary choices has been welcomed by many who have despaired of salvation through society after witnessing the spectacle of two global wars within one lifetime.

Not all phenomenologists, however, agree with such a position of negation and solipsism. Many see the true being of the human person as achievable only in genuine transcendence through community, and they have made a strong case for man as essentially social. In some instances, the inspiration behind this position lies in the Christian notion of man's destiny as one of love and communion with God and his fellow men. The phenomenology of intersubjectivity found in the works of the French philosoper Gabriel Marcel, for example, stems from such a Christian view. The merits of this religiously motivated standpoint we shall not here examine.

In this section, rather, we shall turn to a theory of human community whose inspiration is more clearly philosophical than religious. It is the interpretation advanced by one of the early leaders in the German phenomenological movement, Max Scheler, a philosopher whose orientation is directly opposite to that of Sartre.[1] If Sartre is the prophet of the isolated individual, Scheler is the philosopher of "man-in-community."

[1] The only comprehensive survey in English of Scheler's work is Manfred Frings, *Max Scheler,* Pittsburgh, Duquesne U. Press, 1965. A more lengthy study is Maurice

As a phenomenologist, Scheler differs from Husserl is two major respects: In the first place, Scheler, like many of the early phenomenologists, never followed Husserl's movement from "eidetic" phenomenology to transcendental phenomenology. His basic position is thus realistic rather than idealistic. Consequently, his thinking on intersubjectivity does not become entangled, as does Husserl's, with the problem of epistemologically "justifying" the existence of the other subject – a problem that plagued Husserl's thought and met uncertain resolution in his famous *Cartesian Meditations.* In the second place, Husserl's major phenomenological concern was the analysis of what we might call the purely "rational" structures of man's experience. Scheler, on the contrary, was almost totally taken up with the detection and identification of the non-rational essences in experience. His eidetic phenomenology was directed at discovering the invariant structures in emotional life. Not the world of neutral, "scientic" laws, but the world of values, of the affective and the social, with its own special kinds of laws, was his paramount concern. He worked therefore in an area that Husserl had left virtually untouched, and an area that seemed especially suited to the new method. "Husserl's own phenomenological investigations were, it is true, chiefly logical, epistemological, and to a certain extent ontological. Still, phenomenology, even as he conceived it, is at its persuasive best in the realm of values."[2]

Where Husserl felt the need to show phenomenologically that intersubjective relationships were possible and thus that man was definitely social, Scheler started with this fact as if it were the most basic feature of experience. Behind all his studies in ethics, sociology of knowledge, philosophy of religion and phenomenology of intersubjective, affective participation, his underlying inspiration is the reality of man's social nature. In his mind, community is so essential to man that the social dimension is a truly constitutive factor of man's very being. Man has a social a priori. But it has scarcely been discussed, much less explored, until modern times.

Consequently, Scheler sees the problem of intersubjectivity as one of the ultimate questions in any examination of the foundations of the social sciences. For, "the question of our grounds for assuming the reality of other selves, and the possibility and limits of our understanding of them, is virtually *the* problem for any theory of knowledge in the social sciences."[3]

Dupuy, *La Philosophie de Max Scheler. Son Evolution et Son Unité.* 2 vols., Paris, Presses Universitaires, 1959. A very complete bibliography is available: Wilfred Hartmann, *Max Scheler – Bibliographie,* Frommann Verlag, Stuttgart, 1965.

[2] Quentin Lauer, *Phenomenology: Its Genesis and Prospect,* N. Y. Harper (Torchbook), 1965, p. 10.

[3] Max Scheler, *The Nature of Sympathy,* trans. Peter Heath, London, Routledge & Kegan Paul, 1954, p. xlix.

This is not to say, however, that Scheler's own solutions are equal to the problem, for despite his genius in analyzing the social structure of man, Scheler seems ultimately to have gone to too extreme a position toward a form of pan-vitalism as the final framework of man's social being.

We have already seen in our examination of Sartre's theory that his denial of the possibility of true community between persons stemmed directly from his views on man as arbitrary freedom, who creates both himself and his values by his free choice. Since the human reality for him is, ontologically speaking a "decompression" of universal being, we are not surprised that he should regard man's drive toward community as an attempt forever doomed to frustration. Logic requires a certain reciprocity between one's concept of the subject and one's theory of intersubjectivity. The position that Sartre takes on the nature of the subject clearly determined the analysis which he later advances on the possibility of genuine community. We find this rule of person-community reciprocity exemplified in the work of Scheler no less than in that of Sartre. Consequently, in order to discuss Scheler's theories on the relationships between the self and the other, we must first explain the unique concept of *Person* that he had previously arrived at. After this we shall be in a better position to understand how some aspects of his theory of intersubjectivity developed as they did, under the requirements imposed by his philosophy of *Person*.[4]

With Scheler, as with most philosophers, his general philosophical orientation and interest greatly affects the specific meaning of his major categories. Scheler's early philosophical orientation was primarily ethical. We shall therefore, approach his philosophy of *Person* through his ethical works, for it was while tracing back his ethical discoveries to their center within man that he was led to formulate and elaborate his precise concept of *Person*. The plan of his major ethical work reveals how he arrived at his notion of *Person*. Only after an exhaustive analysis of the foundations of his new ethics does Scheler outline the structure of the *Person* required by this new ethics. It then becomes evident that his concept of *Person* is drawn up in accordance with the requirements of the preceding ethical theory. When Scheler consequently comes to discuss interpersonal relationships, the peculiar structure of man which he has thus derived leads to difficulties which are rooted in some features of his concept of *Person*.

Beyond this, there is a basic and intense polarization in Scheler's thought between the two major categories of spirit and life (*Geist* and *Leben*).

[4] Whenever this word appears capitalized and in italics it refers to Scheler's specific concept which is quite a distinctive one.

Thus, we find that in addition to his stress on man as *Person,* and therefore as a dweller in the realm of *Geist,* Scheler has an equal insistence on man as a dweller in the realm of *Leben.* The life-philosophy of Nietzsche, Bergson and others influenced him to combine his unusual form of personalism (stressing the utter individuality and uniqueness of the *Person*) with an equally insistent pan-vitalism (in which all men are seen as participating in a common life-stream). How Scheler attempts to reconcile these two tendencies and to what extent he succeeds, we shall see as we proceed.

Since Scheler's concept of *Person* was developed in conjunction with his new ethics we can best appreciate his notion of *Person* if we see it emerging from the background of his ethical work. In his later study of intersubjectivity Scheler notes that he was aware of and concerned with the problem of interpersonal relationships during the composition of his major ethical work: "That the solution of the axiological problem as to the relation of individual and community necessarily involves a settlement of this question [how and within what limits we can know and relate to other persons] both on its ontological and epistemological sides,is clearly pointed out in my own *Formalismus in der Ethik.*"[5] Because his ethical theory exercised such a dominant influence on his developing thought about intersubjectivity, we shall briefly outline the major points of his novel value-ethics. After that we shall note some of the essential characteristics that he assigned to the *Person,* characteristics that Scheler believed necessary in order to render man capable of being a center of ethical acts.

It is regrettable that Scheler's ethical work is almost unknown in the English-speaking world, for Scheler manifests the insight of true genius in ethics and social philosophy.

Scheler's major ethical study is a huge tome *Formalism in Ethics and the Material Value-Ethics.*[6] As the title indicates the book had a double purpose: 1) to refute the Kantian "formalistic" ethics; and 2) to outline the foundations of a new "material" value-ethic. The new ethic which Scheler proposes is based upon objective values rather than upon the Kantian subjective imperative; he thus replaces the Kantian insistence on the "form" of ethical judgments by emphasizing the "matter" of ethical acts.

[5] Scheler, *Sympathy,* p. 214. "Dass auch die Lösung der axiologischen Probleme des Verhältnisses von Individuum und Gemeinschaft eine Lösung dieser Frage sowohl nach ihrer ontisch-metaphysischen Seite als nach ihrer erkenntnis-theoretischen notwendig in sich schliesst, hatte ich in meinem Buche uber den 'Formalismus in der Ethik' gelegentlich der Begründung . . . deutlich hervorgehoben." *Wesen und Formen der Sympathie,* 5 ed., Frankfurt, Schulte-Bulmke, 1948, p. 229.

[6] *Der Formalismus in der Ethik und die materiale Wertethik,* 5 ed., Bern, Francke Verlag, 1966. There is presently no English translation, though one is in preparation by Northwestern University Press. Quotations in the text are the writer's translation. The German original is given in the footnotes.

Scheler undertakes his criticism of the Kantian ethic by attacking the basic premise on which it rests. If ethics is to be universal and absolute, said Kant, it must be based upon an a priori subjective principle, and furthermore, this principle must be purely formal, because all material elements are a posteriori derivations and as such are merely contingent and relative. The identification "a priori = subjective formal" and "a posteriori = material" is one of the foundation stones upon which Kant's two critiques of knowledge are built. It is, says Scheler, the principiating error of the entire Kantian position. "Taking the 'a priori' factor as identical with the 'formal' factor is a *basic error* of Kant's system. It is at the basis of ethical 'formalism' and indeed of his over-all 'formal idealism' – as Kant calls his system."[7]

By refuting this principle Scheler clears the ground for his own ethical theory which will be objectively a priori and material. The establishment of the objective values as the basis for ethics simultaneously demolishes transcendental subjectivism as a point of departure for ethics.

A second presupposition of Kantian ethics which must be destroyed in order to make way for Scheler's value ethics is the principle that since the *material* element is related to *sense,* the *formal* element concerns only the purely "rational." This second principle of Kant's is intimately related to the one just mentioned: "Closely connected with the first is another basic principle. I refer to the principle that (both in his theory of knowledge as well as in his ethics) equates the 'material' factor with *'sensory'* content and the 'a priori' factor with the *'rational'*."[8]

Kant's adherence to this distinction is responsible for his refusal to ascribe any importance to the material aspect of ethics. Since he holds that every material (empirical) determination of the will would necessarily be through sense, such a will would be referred only to pleasure and pain as motives for action. On such a relative foundation, says Kant, no ethics could be erected, for ethics must be universal and undetermined by contingent events. Kant's principle is false, declares Scheler, for the "materiality" of the thing presented to the will has nothing to do with sense-perception or aposteriority: "All acts of willing have some *'material content'* as a foundation. This 'matter', however, can be a priori, and is so whenever it

[7] "Die Identifizierung des 'Apriorischen' mit dem 'Formalen' ist ein *Grundirrtum* der Kantischen Lehre. Er liegt auch dem ethischen 'Formalismus' mit zugrunde, ja dem 'formalen Idealismus' – wie Kant selbst seine Lehre nennt – überhaupt. *Form.,* p. 73.

[8] "Mit ihm hängt ein anderer aufs engste zusammen. Ich meine die Gleichsetzung des 'Materialen' (sowohl in der Theorie der Erkenntnis als in der Ethik) mit dem *'sinnlichen'* Gehalt, des 'Apriorischen' aber mit dem *'Gedachten.'"* *Form.,* p. 73.

is *value-qualities* that determine the receptivity of the will. Such acts of willing are therefore not in the least determined by sensory-based feelings."[9]

Kant, however, is led by his error concerning the sense derivation of the material element to declare his basic ethical principle, that the ethical imperative can be nothing but a law of "reason." The categorical imperative is thus revealed as a pure form of judgment analogous to the theoretical categories outlined in the *Critique of Pure Reason* but differing from them by the object which is subsumed under its form. Just as Kant had equated sense perception with material and declared both a posteriori, so he has also equated formal with a priori and declared all a priori elements to be functions of the understanding. What results therefore is an "intellectual ethics," ruled by the empty form of the ethical imperative.

Scheler's theory of ethics is opposed to Kantian ethics on every major point. His starting point is fundamentally different: he does away with transcendental idealism and takes a rigorous realism as his basic position. This general philosophical orientation determines much that follows in his ethics. The rule of the subjective imperative is replaced by the "ought" of the objective values; Kant's preoccupation with the formal element is replaced by Scheler's insistence on the material factor; the exaggerated role assigned to the intellectual a priori is replaced by the emotional a priori of the sense of values.

Scheler's criticism of some of these points has been indicated above. His refutation is not in all respects unprecedented. With the theory of the emotional a priori, however, we come to the most distinctive and original contribution of Scheler to ethical research. This, together with the thesis on the objective values, constitutes the heart of the new ethics. It was while working out the function of the emotional factor and its correlative object that Scheler was led to propose his original and unique theory of the structure of the ethical person.

Kant's failure to realize the presence of the emotional a priori because of his uncritical belief that all a priori was necessarily of purely intellectual dimensions is the last error which Scheler enumerates. It is not, however, any less important in the ultimate structure of the Kantian ethics: "Another, and no less serious error results from the equating of the 'a priori' factor with the 'rational,' of an 'a priori position' with 'rationalism' – a

[9] "Und eben ... hat alles Wollen eine Fundierung in *Materien;* die gleichwohl a priori sein können, sofern sie in *Wertqualitäten* bestehen, nach denen sich erst die *Bildinhalte* des Wollens bestimmen. Das Wollen ist *darum* nicht im mindesten durch 'sinnliche Gefühlszustände' bestimmt." *Form.*, p. 81.

position that Kant proposes, and that works to the detriment of ethics."[10]

What Scheler now demands is a readmission of the emotional factor into the ethical sphere. The old prejudice that everything emotional was derived from and connected with the sense order and hence inadmissable as ethical matter, can no longer be sustained. The restriction of "pure" acts to the domain of the understanding is the Kantian error that must be corrected. "That is to say, *'pure'* acts, and laws governing these acts, are found in the *entire* sphere of the life of spirit, and not merely in the area that deals with being through objective knowledge and thought."[11]

Scheler proposes therefore to give to the emotional side of man its proper role "What we, therefore, most emphatically demand – in contrast to Kant – is *an apriority of the emotional,* and a sundering of the false unity that till now has existed between the a priori and the rational."[12] Such an emotional a priori would be characterized by the presence of acts which, in their independence from the sense sphere, would be in no way less "pure" than those of "pure thought," but which because of their evaluative and preferential tension would be irreducible to intellectual acts. Does there not exist, asks Scheler, *"pure perception and feeling, pure love and hatred, pure striving and willing,* all of which taken together, are as independent of the psycho-physical structure of the human being as is pure thinking"?[13] The search for such emotional acts which would be independent of the sense sphere, has not received much attention from previous philosophers, says Scheler, but among the few who have studied the problem are two outstanding names: "I list among them Augustine and Blaise Pascal."[14]

Does such a sphere of acts exist? Scheler replies with an emphatic affirmative: "Those acts of the spirit, such as feeling, preference, love and hatred, have their own *a priori* content which is as independent of inductive experience as are the laws of pure thinking."[15] In attempting to clarify

[10] "Aber noch in eine andere, nicht minder tiefe Irrung gerät die Gleichsetzung des 'Apriorischen' mit dem 'Gedachten,' des 'Apriorismus' mit dem 'Rationalismus,' wie Kant ihn – besondere zum Schaden der Ethik – vertritt." *Form.*, p. 82.

[11] "Es ist nämlich unser *ganzes* geistiges Leben – nicht bloss das gegenständliche Erkennen und Denken im Sinne der Seinserkenntnis – das *'reine'* ... Akte und Aktgesetze hat." *Form.*, p. 82.

[12] "Was wir also – gegenüber Kant – hier entschieden fordern, ist ein *Apriorismus des Emotionalen* und eine Scheidung der falschen *Einheit,* die bisher zwischen Apriorismus und Rationalismus bestand." *Form.*, p. 84.

[13] *"ein reines Anschauen, Fühlen, ein reines Lieben und Hassen, ein reines Streben und Wollen* ... die all zusammen von der psychophysischen Organisation unserer Menschenart *ebenso* unabhängig sind, wie das reine Denken ..." *Form.*, p. 259.

[14] "Ich nenne unter ihnen Augustin und Blaise Pascal." *Form.*, p. 260.

[15] "Das Fühlen, das Vorziehen, das Lieben und Hassen des Geistes hat seinen eige-

what he means by the emotional a priori, Scheler refers to the Pascalian "logique du coeur." As Pascal had found Cartesian rationalism inadequate to the concrete situations of life, Scheler finds the Kantian practical judgment a shallow attempt to explain the richness of concrete moral situations which reveal upon analysis, not only cognitive, but preferential and emotional factors that are inescapable. Nicolai Hartmann, in his *Ethics,* based upon Scheler's work, has insisted upon this same uniqeness of the moral act. He echoes Scheler here:

> In our concrete moral life there is as little of such a subsuming function of judgment as there is in the natural concrete knowledge of things. Every moral preference is intuitive, is immediately there and is always contained in the grasping of a given circumstance (whether it be a situation or a finished course of conduct). It does not first wait for a judgment of the understanding. Comprehension of ethical reality – whether it consist of goods, human relations or demands for a personal decision – is always, even for the naivest consciousness, transfused with valuations, with preferences in accordance with feeling, with strong tensions for and against. All acts which are related to this fulness of life and which grasp reality are at the same time acts which grasp values and which select according to values. But as such they are never purely cognitive acts; they are acts of feeling – not intellectual but emotional.[16]

There are such pure emotional acts, and it is with them that ethics must deal says Scheler. They are the distinctive acts of the spiritual center of man: "The *emotional dimension* of spirit – feeling, preferring, loving, hating, and willing – has an *original a priori content* which it does not borrow from the realm of 'thinking' and which ethics has shown to be quite independent of logic. There is an a priori 'ordre du coeur' or 'logique du coeur' as Blaise Pascal succinctly phrases it."[17]

The *logique du coeur* therefore indicates a type of experience whose objects are specifically correlated to the emotional side of man, objects which can in no way be apprehended by the faculty of understanding. "There is a type of experience whose objects are completely alien to the understanding, for which the understanding is as uncomprehending as the ear and the auditory sense is blind to color; a type of experience, however, which provides us with 'objects' that are *genuinely* objective and are

nen *apriorischen* Gehalt, der von der induktiven Erfahrung so unabhängig ist, wie die reinen Denkengesetze." *Form.,* p. 84.

[16] Nicolai Hartmann, *Ethics,* trans. Stanton Coit, 3 vols., N.Y. Macmillan, 1932, Vol. I, p. 176–7.

[17] "... das *Emotionale* des Geistes, das Fühlen, Vorziehen, Lieben, Hassen, Wollen, hat einen *ursprünglichen apriorischen Gehalt,* den es nicht vom 'Denken' erborgt, und den die Ethik ganz unabhängig von der Logik aufzuweisen hat. Es gibt eine apriorische 'Ordre du coeur' oder 'logique du coeur' wie Blaise Pascal treffend sagt." *Form.,* p. 82.

ranked in a fixed order; these are *the values* and the hierarchy that exists among them."[18]

The discovery of the importance of the emotional side of man has led Scheler to the realization that man approaches the world not merely as an intellectual being endowed with categories for "understanding" the manifold of sense, but as a being endowed with an a priori "sense of value," a capacity for discovering in things their individual worth and importance. This "sense of value" is not identical with speculative knowledge; neither is it the same as the subjectively imposed Kantian imperative. Rather it is an emotional insight into the hierarchy of values existing in the real order.

> The true source of every a priori value is the *value-awareness* and *value- perception* stemming from feeling, preference, and ultimately from love and hatred, just as awareness of the interrelationship of values – of their being 'higher' or 'lower' – is based on moral perception. This kind of perception, consequently, evolves in *specific* functions and acts, acts which are utterly different from every other type of perception and thinking, and acts which constitute the only possible *access* to the world of values. Not through 'inner perception' or observation (in which only the psychical is given), but rather *in* the lived, felt intercourse with the world (be it psychical or physical or of any other kind), *in* loving and *in* hating itself, in the very *fulfillment* of those intentional acts – it is here that the values and their hierarchical order shine forth.[19]

By his discovery of the a priori value feeling and the correlative realm of values which address themselves to men, Scheler re-establishes ethics on a new basis. The ethics of intellectualistic formalism which reached its highest expression in Kant is replaced by an emotional material ethics. In place of the "ought" of the empty categorical imperative man is bound by the summons (*Ruf*) of the objective values, which are given to him in the intentional feeling as colors are given in the act of seeing. This is the new center in man which Scheler reveals. It is not to be identified with in-

[18] "Es gibt eine Erfahrungsart, deren Gegenstände dem 'Verstande' völlig verschlossen sind; für die dieser so blind ist wie Ohr und Hören fur die Farbe, eine Erfahrungsart aber, die uns *echte* objective Gegenstände und eine ewige Ordnung zwischen ihnen zuführt, eben *die Werte*; und eine Rangordnung zwischen ihnen." *Form.*, p. 261.

[19] "Der eigentliche Sitz alles Wertapriori . . . ist die im Fühlen, Vorziehen, in letzter Linie im Lieben und Hassen sich aufbauende *Werterkenntnis* resp. *Werterschauung,* sowie die der Zusammenhänge der Werte, ihres 'Höher' und 'Niedriger-seins,' d.h. die '*sittliche* Erkenntnis.' Diese Erkenntnis erfolgt also in *spezifischen* Funktionen und Akten, die von allem Wahrnehmen und Denken toto caelo verschieden sind und den einzig möglichen *Zugang* zur Welt der Werte bilden. Nicht durch 'innere Wahrnehmung' oder Beobachtung (in der ja nur Psychisches gegeben ist), sondern *im* fühlenden, lebendigen Verkehr mit der Welt (sei sie psychisch oder physisch oder was sonst), *im* Lieben und Hassen selbst, d.h. in der Linie des *Vollzuges* jener intentionalen Akte blitzen die Werte und ihre Ordnungen auf!" *Form.*, p. 87.

tellect, for the intellect is as "blind" to the perception of values as the ear is to colors.

The consequences of his ethical theory of values upon Scheler's concept of man and his unique theory of *Person*, are very great. We shall at this point, therefore, indicate the main characteristics which he assigns to man as the "ethical being." His analysis of the various psychic levels within the human being pre-determines his theory of interpersonal relationships to a great extent. In particular, his distinction between *Ich* (Ego) and *Person* is basic for his later researches into intersubjectivity. For this reason we shall now examine Scheler's concept of *Person*. The intimate connection between the value ethics which we have sketched briefly and the notion of *Person* will then become apparent.

The Distinction of Person and Ego

The emotional a priori which Scheler discovered in his research into value ethics was characterized by independence from the sense sphere. In order to account for this phenomenon, he concluded, there must be a psychic center in man superior to the whole realm of the vital. Thus he was led to an analysis of man into different psychic levels. Two general categories emerged, that of the *Person* and that of the Ego. These became basic for Scheler's later theory of intersubjectivity. In the course of time he elaborated his analyses, and it is from one of his later works that the main distinctions may most easily be grasped.

According to the scheme of philosophical anthropology which Scheler outlined in *Man's Place in Nature,* man is a being who stands on the topmost rung of a five-stage order of nature. Below man, existence in the world is found in four steps: 1) unconscious, insensate, vegetable life; 2) instinctive life of lower animals; 3) associative memory or the life of "conditioned reflex actions;" 4) practical intelligence, or the life of animal adaptability to environmental changes.[20]

Man, as a being in the vital sphere, shares in all these lower realms of psychic existence. As a being in this sphere he can be studied by the methods of experimental psychology. The complexus of all these vital psychic centers within the human being, Scheler designates as the Ego. The activities of the Ego he calls "functions," such as seeing, tasting, bodily feelings; "functions" include a reference to the bodily sphere. The vital sphere is thus the domain of the incarnate subject. The Ego is characterized also by

[20] Max Scheler, *Man's Place in Nature,* trans. Hans Meyerhoff, N.Y., Farrar, Straus, 1961, pp. 8–34. A translation of: *Die Stellung des Menschen im Kosmos,* Darmstadt, Otto Reichl-Verlag, 1929, p. 16–39.

the fact that it can be made object of knowledge or of a reflective act. "The Ego . . . is in every sense of the word still an object; Ego-hood is an object of unstructured intuition, and the individual Ego is an object of inner perception."[21]

Apart from the Ego however, Scheler has distinguished a higher dimension of man. Specifically as man, he is constituted by a principle which entirely surpasses the vital sphere and which consequently is beyond the scope of experimental psychology, and beyond all objectification. This principle Scheler calls *"Geist." Geist* (Spirit) is not only the root of "reason," but also the foundation for those powers specifically ordained to the perception of essences and to the performance of certain types of emotional and volitive acts, such as those of love, kindness, awe, repentance. The active center in man that possesses this being of *Geist,* is what Scheler calls *Person.*

The *Person* is thus totally above the realm of the lower psychic centers in man. The specific attribute distinguishing it from them is its freedom from its environment, even from the "environment" of the subordinate spheres of man. Because of *Geist,* man is raised above the mere animal consciousness to the plane of self-consciousness; because of it he may *objectify* even his own experiences, physical and psychical, a power unknown to animals. This power of the acts of the *Person* to deal with both the physical and psychical spheres while remaining superior to both Scheler calls "the psycho-physical indifference of acts. This is clearly shown by the fact that all acts and different kinds of acts can have as objects something psychical as well as physical."[22]

But this center of man, the *Person,* is so eminent that it can never become object, for that which makes objects possible for man cannot itself be subject to the conditions of objectivity. Neither the *Person* nor his specific acts, therefore, can be made "objects" of knowledge. For the *Person* only exists in the performance of his acts, and since the acts can never be objects of knowledge, neither can their principle. Scheler says: "As an act is never an object, neither is the living, act-fulfilling *Person* ever object."[23] If the act cannot be made object, neither can the *Person,* for "it belongs

[21] "Das 'Ich . . . ist in jedem Sinne de Wortes noch ein Gegenstand; die Ichheit noch ein Gegenstand formloser Anschauung, das individuelle Ich ein Gegenstand innerer Wahrnehmung." *Form.,* p. 386.

[22] "Die psychophysice Indifferenz der Akte . . . kommt darin scharf zur Gegebenheit, dass alle Akte und Aktunterschiede ebensowohl Psychisches wie Physisches zum Gegenstande haben können." *Form.,* p. 390.

[23] "Ist aber schon ein Akt niemals Gegenstand, so ist recht niemals Gegenstand die in ihrem Aktvollzug lebende *Person.*" *Form.,* p. 386.

to the very *essence* of the *Person* that he exists and lives only *in the fulfillment of intentional acts.* It is thus of the essence of *Person* that he can never be an object."[24]

If we cannot make objects of our acts and our inner core, the *Person,* how can we possibly know of them. Scheler replies that we grasp our acts by a concomitant awareness or simultaneous reflection, which however in no way makes the act an *object* in the full sense. "An act is never an object because it belongs to the being of acts to be experienced only in fulfillment and given only in reflection. One act can never become an object by means of a second retrospective act. For even in the reflection that makes the act cognizant of its (naive) fulfillment, this latter is never object; the reflexive awareness accompanies the act, but never objectifies it."[25]

Scheler's view on the nature of *Person* and Ego were greatly influenced, as were his ethical views, by his criticism of Kantian teaching. The dissolution of the concrete existing individual into the transcendental unity of apperception was one of Kant's grave errors according to Scheler. Emphasizing the role of the *Person* as the existing ethical being, Scheler criticizes the empty unity which Kant subsituted as a mere "starting point" for the activity of reason. The Kantian "subject" is not a person but merely a form binding the diverse of perception into a unity. But we can easily imagine, says Scheler, beings capable *only* of reasoning or *only* of willing and their corresponding acts; such beings would in no sense be *Persons.* "Such beings would be still (logical) subjects performing rational acts. But they would not be *Persons* .... Exactly the same situation would prevail if we had beings capable only of accomplishing acts of willing. They would be (logical) subjects of will – but they would not be *Persons.*"[26]

Such a view of the *Person* would be a de-personalization of the *Person.* The *Person* through his acts is not a mere unifier of sense perception, not a merely logical necessity arrived at by the Kantian regressive method as the ultimate necessary condition that there be any experience at all possi-

[24] "... *zum Wesen der Person gehört,* dass sie nur existiert und lebt *im Vollzug intentionaler Akte.* Sie ist also wesenhaft kein 'Gegenstand.'" *Form.,* p. 389.

[25] 'Niemals aber ist ein Akt auch ein Gegenstand; denn es gehört zum Wesen des Seins von Akten nur im Vollzug selbst erlebt und in Reflexion gegeben zu sein. Niemals kann mithin ein Akt durch einen zweiten, etwa rückblickenden Akt wieder Gegenstand werden. Denn auch in der Reflexion, die den Akt über seinen (naiven) Vollzug hinaus noch wissbar macht, ist er niemals 'Gegenstand;' das reflexive Wissen 'begleitet' ihn, aber vergegenständlicht ihn nicht." *Form.,* p. 374.

[26] "Diese Wesen wären immer noch (logische) Subjekte, die Vernunftakte vollzögen: Aber 'Personen' wären sie nicht .... Genau dasselbe galte aber auch von Wesen, denen alle Inhalte nur als Projekte im Wollen gegeben waren. Sie wären (logische) Subjekte eines Wollens – aber keine Personen." *Form.,* p. 382.

ble. Scheler protests vigorously against all such abstract and purely rationalistic views of the person.

His previous research into the concrete material value-ethics has brought him to the conclusion the the *Person* is a concrete, existing, value-feeling being whose highest acts are entirely above and superior to the whole order of sense perception and the laws of its unification. The *Person* is a spiritual center deep within man, the basis of essentially different acts, and totally independent of the whole vital sphere. *Person* is a being in the realm of spirit *(Geist)*. In speaking of "the psychophysical indifference" characteristic both of the *Person* and his acts, Scheler sets forth his essential definition of *Person*:

> The *Person* is *the concrete, essentially undivided unity-of-being that pervades the multiplicity and variety of human acts.* This unity-of-being is really, and not merely logically, prior to all that subsequent differentiation which arises from the fact that acts are of essentially different kinds; (such as the noteworthy difference between the external and internal dimensions of perception, of willing, of feeling, of loving and hating, etc.). *The being of the Person serves as the unified source from which all these acts, despite their essential differences, stem.*[27]

Contrary to the Kantian idea of the subject standing necessarily behind all knowledge as the ultimate (logical) condition of any experience, the *Person* is not a static unity "behind" or "beyond" his acts. On the contrary the *Person* as a whole is involved in each concrete act, and exists only in his acts. "The *Person* exists only the fulfillment of his acts:"[28] "The *Person* is continuous actuality."[29] This does not mean that the *Person* is merely a collection of acts, but rather that the *Person,* living in each of his acts, without being absorbed by them, suffuses each one with his specific individuality. "Rather, the entire *Person* is embedded in *every* completely concrete act; and thus the *entire Person* 'varies' by being *in* and expressing himself *through* each different act, without exhausting his being-potential in any one act, or becoming essentially changed as a nonpersonal thing would be if subjected to analogous temporal variation."[30]

[27] "*Person ist die konkrete, selbst wesenhafte Seinseinheit von Akten verschiedenartigen Wesens,* die an sich (nicht also πρὸς ἡμᾶς) allen wesenhaften Aktdifferenzen (insbesondere auch der Differenz äusserer und innerer Wahrnehmung, äusseren und inneren Wollens, äusseren und inneren Fühlen und Liebens, Hassens, usw.) vorhergeht. *Das Sein der Person 'fundiert' alle wesenhaft verschiedenen Akte.*" *Form.*, p. 383.

[28] "Sie existiert nur im Vollzug ihrer Akte." *Form.*, p. 51.

[29] "Person ist kontinuierliche Aktualität." *Form.*, p. 103, n. 1.

[30] "Vielmehr steckt in *jedem* voll konkreten Akt die *ganze Person* und *'variiert'* in

From the foregoing description of *Person* we can see more clearly the basic distinction which Scheler introduces betweeen this spiritual center of man and the lower psychic center which he designates as Ego. Whereas psychology in studying "personality" depends upon those features of man which can be observed and described, Scheler declares that any study of the *Person* in such a way is impossible. The *Person* is never an "object" for observation. *Person* is spirit and transcends all such perception. What psychology may and does study is rather the Ego. "The *Person* can ... become aware of his own Ego, as in the study of psychology."[31] This is possible because the activities of the Ego are "functions" which include a reference to the body. The "acts" of the *Person,* on the other hand, are completely "indifferent" to both psychical and physical spheres. For Scheler, however, as we have seen it is characteristic of the essence of the *Person* to exist and live only in the performance of intentional acts; the performance of psychical "functions" has no importance in treating of the *Person.* Psychology, as it is at present understood, therefore, never reaches the realm of the spiritual *Person.* "If we understand by '*consciousness*' everything that appears before inner perception (as when we define psychology as the science of the phenomena of consciousness), then the *Person* and his acts must be designated as *supra-conscious being.*"[32]

The *Person,* in Scheler's view, is not a static essence merely existing to perform certain acts, however spiritual. Rather does the *Person* undergo a development through the performance of moral acts. Indeed, in the beginning, the *Person* exists in each man only "in germ," so to speak. The *Person* is directed essentially toward moral values in order to develop into a complete *Person* by act-responses to these values, for man stands not only in a cognitive relation to the objective sphere of values by his special faculty of emotional "value-feeling," but he stands in a correlative practical relation to them insofar as they "demand" his response, and carry the note of "oughtness."

For each man there exists, says Scheler, a specific ideal value-person which he is called upon to achieve. He is to achieve this by his response to those values which have a special ordering toward him, for the values do

und durch jeden Akt auch die ganze Person – ohne dass ihr Sein doch in irgendeinem ihrer Akte aufginge, oder sich wie ein Ding in der Zeit 'veränderte.'" *Form.,* p. 384.

[31] "Eine Person kann ... auch ihr Ich 'wahrnehmen,' z.B. wenn sie Psychologie treibt." *Form.,* p. 389.

[32] "Verstehen wir unter dem Worte '*Bewusstsein*' ... alles in innerer Wahrnehmung in die Erscheinung Tretende, so wie es geschieht, wenn man Psychologie z.B. als 'Wissenschaft von den Bewusstseinserscheinungen' definiert, so muss die *Person* und müssen ihre Akte als *überbewusstes Sein* bezeichnet werden." *Form.,* p. 391.

not exist "in general" and are not presented to all men in the same way. This does not mean that each man *makes* his own values, in the subjectivistic sense of ethical relativism, a position which we have seen Sartre carry to the logical extreme. Rather it means for Scheler that in the whole realm of objective values possible of realization by someone, a special "set" or complexus of values is presented to each *Person* as the way in which he must achieve the actualization of his specific *Person*-value, for "even given a similar organic, psychic, and environmental situation, each *Person*, ethically considered, comports himself differently and is related to different ethical values."[33]

This full development of his "personality" appears before each one not only as something which *may* be achieved, but as something which *should* be achieved, as something which makes its demands felt. Scheler describes the demands of the specific *Person*-value as a "call," an "appeal":

> ... whose accompanying 'ought' occurs, therefore, as a 'call' to this *Person* and to him alone, regardless of whether or not this same call is made to others. Here there occurs that recognition of the essential value of *my Person* (in religious language we could call it the value-image which the love of God for me has established, designated and allotted), of *my* specific, individual value-capability as the ground of this individual ought. In short, it is clear recognition of a good that is simultaneously 'good-in-itself' and also 'good-for-*me*'.[34]

This designation of "good-for-me" is in no way contradictory with its also being a value independent of me for its existence, a thing important in itself. The further designation of it as "for me" merely indicates that the special material content of this particular good includes, as Scheler says so strikingly: "an experience of, as it were, a finger pointing toward me from the depths of this value, as if it were whispering 'for you.' The specific content of this individual value assigns me a unique place in the ethical cosmos, and it commands also the performance of actions, deeds, and works, all of them crying out 'I am for you,' and 'You are for me.'"[35]

[33] "... jede Person unter sonst gleichen organischen, psychischen und äusseren Umständen von jeder anderen Person sich ethisch verschieden und verschiedenwertig verhalten." *Form.*, p. 500.

[34] "... dessen zugehöriges Sollen daher als ein 'Ruf' an diese Person und sie allein ergeht, gleichgültig ob derselbe 'Ruf' auch an andere ergehe oder nicht. Das ist also das Erblicken des Wesenswertes *meiner Person* – in religiöser Sprache, des Wertbildes, das die Liebe Gottes, sofern sie auf mich gerichtet ist, von mir gleichsam hat und vor mich hinzeichnet und vor mir beträgt, – dieser eigenarte individuelle Wertgehalt, auf den sich erst das Bewusstsein des individuellen Sollens aufbaut, d.h. es ist evidente Erkenntnis eines An-Sich-Guten, aber eben des 'an-Sich-Guten für *mich*.'" *Form.*, p. 482.

[35] "... ein erlebter Fingerzeig, der von diesem *Gehalte* ausgeht und auf 'mich'

The task of developing one's spiritual "personality" through a proper response to the ethical values is not one that once accepted, is thereby completed. Every situation in life presents us with new values offered for our acceptance. Some of these values are entirely specific to each *Person,* and once presented for choice, may never again be offered; if refused they are lost for eternity. It is the task of each *Person* therefore to develop his value perception and to respond correctly to the values that continually offer themselves to him through life.

Every vital moment in the whole series of events and situations that enter into the development of the individual offers never-to-be-repeated opportunities for grasping specific and unique values, and for performing ethical tasks and actions that can never be possible again. These ethical acts are, as it were, predetermined for this moment (and perhaps for this individual), in the objective context of the independently-existing order of ethical values; and if these acts are not performed, the possibility for actualizing the values inherent in them is lost for eternity.[36]

In concluding this discussion of Scheler's distinction of *"Person"* and Ego we may summarize the main lines of it as follows. Working within an ethical framework, Scheler finds in man a center of ethical acts, which center is independent of the whole sensory order and ordained specifically to spiritual "acts." This center he called *Person.* Among other characteristics of *Person* is the emotional value-feeling directed at the objective order of values, by response to which the *Person* develops toward the ideal value-essence for which his "personality" was destined. Below the level of *Person* lies the sphere of the Ego. In contradistinction to the *Person,* the Ego can be made object of knowledge. It is the center of the vital functions of man. Study of its functions, however, contributes nothing to the knowledge of the *Person* himself, for the *Person* and the acts of the *Person* are never "objects" for knowledge.

Scheler has introduced, as we see, a great and basic distinction in the very essential constitution of the human being. In his endeavor to provide

deutet; das gleichsam sagt und flüstert: 'für dich.' Und dieser *Gehalt* weist mir damit eine einzigartige Stelle im sittlichen Kosmos an und gebietet mir sekundär auch Handlungen, Taten, Werke, die stelle ich sie vor alle rufen: 'Ich bin für dich' und 'Du bist für mich.' " *Form.,* p. 482.

[36] "*. . . stellt jeder Lebensmoment einer individualen Entwickelungsreihe* zugleich die Erkenntnismöglichkeit für ganz bestimmte und *einmalige* Werte und Wertzusammenhange dar, entsprechend dieser aber die Nötigung zu sittlichen Aufgaben und Handlungen, die sich niemals wiederholen können und die im objektiven Nexus der an sich bestehenden sittlichen Wertordnung für diesen Moment (und etwa für dieses Individuum) gleichsam pradeterminiert sind und die, ungenutzt, notwendig für ewig verloren gehen." *Form.,* p. 485.

an objective ethics whose content or "matter" will in no way be reducible to the sense sphere and whose basis will be emotional rather than intellectual, he is led to split the unity of man by establishing the ethical center, the *Person,* beyond the range of "objective" knowledge. This permits him to describe a great hierarchy of values to which different levels of man are ordained, but the sundering of the unity of man is a grave consequence, and it can be questioned whether such a radical division within the human being was as necessary to the success of the value-ethics as Scheler seemed to believe.

While the fruitfulness of the approach to man through a consideration of value cannot be denied, one might hope it possible to develop a theory of value-ethics which does not endanger the intrinsic unity of the human being. As we have noted in Sartre, and as we shall see again, the question of values and man's relation to values seems to be intimately connected with the whole problem of interpersonal relationships. The position which one assigns to values, indeed, determines much that one finds in any theory of the person and his interpersonal relationships. The results of Sartre's and Scheler's basic attitude toward values is instructive in this regard.

From our examination of Scheler's theory of *Person* we are now in a position to advance to a treatment of his theory of intersubjectivity. It will be seen that the distinction of *Person* and Ego which we have explained above is the key to an understanding of his phenomenology of intersubjectivity.

CHAPTER IV

CRITIQUE OF PREVIOUS THEORIES

We have already noted that in his ethical studies, Scheler was intensely interested in determining the structure of man and the living ethical relations which bind man as a social being to other men. The ethical relations of man were not the sole concern of Scheler, however, for his investigations extend into the whole problem of sociality in general and specific social relations in particular. Guided by his analysis of man as a being living in two spheres, the "vital" and the "spiritual," Scheler undertook to give a detailed account of the various types of community in which each man is ontologically engaged.

This resulted in the determination of a great hierarchy of communities extending through the vital up to the highest reaches of the purely spiritual, religious community. The scope of our study, however, does not permit an examination of the whole question of Scheler's general philosophy of community.[1] We are concerned only to indicate the analysis which Scheler makes of that most primary form of community involving one individual person and another. This problem, though narrower, cuts across the divisions of vital and spiritual spheres, as we shall see.

Scheler's most extensive treatment of the problem which concerns us is given in his book *The Nature of Sympathy,* the first volume of a projected series on the structure and laws of emotional life. This book and his ethical work will be our main sources for Scheler's theory of interpersonal relationships.

Conditions for a Solution

Scheler begins his study of the problem of intersubjectivity with a survey of what has been accomplished to date by philosophers and psychologists in

[1] For an excellent survey of Scheler's theory of man as involved in various communities in different ways one can consult Ernest W. Ranly, C.PP. S., *Scheler's Phenomenology of Community,* The Hague, Nijhoff, 1966.

this field. He feels that the reason for the little progress which has been made lies in the failure to distinguish the various points of view from which the entire question may be seen, and the order in which the different sub-problems must be solved. He therefore sets forth six major questions which enter into the constitution of the total problem of interpersonal relationships. Since these questions open up the full range of the problem in a succinct fashion, we shall summarize the six questions and note briefly how Scheler answers them.

1) The ontological problem. What are the essential relations existing between the individual and community in general? Are they correlative in such a way that man's being includes a reference to community as an internal relation, and independently of any concrete man within a concrete community now existing? Furthermore, ought we to admit that the relations existing between men insofar as they are beings in the sphere of "life" are equally as essential as the relations existing between men insofar as they are *Persons* and beings of "spirit?" To all three questions Scheler answers affirmatively.

2) The epistemological problem. By what reason, asks Scheler, do I who write these lines, form real judgments of a) the existence of community in general; b) the existence of another determined Ego; and c) the existence of the *Person* of the other? As we shall see, Scheler answers: a) every man is community-oriented in an essential a priori way; b) I reach the other Ego through the fact that he physically expresses himself; and c) I reach the other *Person* by a "co-performance" of his acts, and thus a participation in his being.

3) The problem of origins. What is the exact sequence in the order of acquiring knowledge of others? Does knowledge of others presuppose knowledge of self? Yes, says Scheler. Does it presuppose that knowledge of self is the primary fact from which we start? Scheler denies it. With respect to his distinction of *Person* and Ego, he holds, as we shall see, that even in the absence of the other, our simple encounter with intelligent signs left by the other would make us aware of the existence of another *Person*. But we come to know another Ego only through his bodily expressive features; for Ego-perception, therefore, the other must be physically present. Another question he raises: Does knowledge of the other *Person* presuppose a knowledge of the exterior, non-living world of nature, are both simultaneous, or does knowledge of nature follow other-*Person* knowledge? Scheler holds for the last position: "So far as the minds of others are concerned we shall find it necessary to accept the third alternative. The only thing we can concede as a prior condition for accomplishment of the act of knowing other

minds is what we may call a sense of the 'ideal meaning of signs' in general."[2]

Whereas evidence of the existence of other *Persons* may be given without their presence, the situation is different when we discuss the other Ego. In this case his physical presence is necessary. But our knowledge of the other Ego is not consequent to our knowledge of dead nature. On the contrary, the first aspect of nature presented to us is the realm of the vital for "our primary knowledge of Nature is itself a knowledge of the *expressive* aspect of living organisms."[3] The realm of life, of the psychical, revealed through the fact of *expression* is our first introduction into nature.

The infant and the true primitive, Scheler declares, have no concept of an exterior "object" (as distinct from psychic "subjects") nor of "dead" being. On the contrary, all reality first presents itself to them as a *single* enormous field of expressions (*ein* grosses Ausdrucksfeld) out from which particular expressions gradually emerge. Therefore Scheler concludes that our knowledge of other Egos is simultaneously given with knowledge of the organic form (e.g. the physical body of man). Our primary knowledge is of the totality, the psychical and physical together. "It is only from the total unity of the 'animate' body that we go on to differentiate our knowledge of our fellow-man into an acquaintance with his physical body on the one hand, and his 'inner life' on the other."[4]

The problem of origins also includes the further question: in what order do we come to know the different social groups? For Scheler, our knowledge of others in any social group presupposes the more direct knowledge of others given in the family, and this itself arose on the basis of an incorporation into the family at an age when this knowledge was not so much knowledge as a real "affective fusion" ("*echte Einsfühlung*") with others which is really a type of "mass" or "herd" participation.

The problem of orgins also asks about the different psychic strata which we penetrate in our knowledge of the other. For Scheler, the inmost is the "intimate" sphere of the *Person* unknowable in its totality, and incommuni-

[2] *Sympathy*, p. 217–18. "Wir glauben uns hinsichtlich 'geistiges Ich' für das dritte Glied der Disjunktion entscheiden zu müssen; nur das, was wir Bestand von 'idealem Zeichensinn' überhaupt nennen können, werden wir als Voraussetzungs-gegebenheit für die Aktualisierung des Aktes von Fremdwissen geistiger Subjekte zulassen." *Sympathie*, p. 233.

[3] *Sympathy*, p. 218. "... unser erstes Wissen um Natur selbst Wissen um *Ausdruck* von Lebewesen ist." *Sympathie*, p. 233.

[4] *Sympathy*, p. 218. "Erst von der Ganzheit des 'beseelten Leibes' geht die Differenzierung des Wissens in einer Richtung zum Leib-Körper – in der andern zu einer 'Innenwelt' des Mitmenschen." *Sympathie*, p. 234.

cable even by a free act of the other. For, like the acts through which it manifests itself, the *Person* is not an "object" of knowledge for another.

These levels or degrees of knowledge of the other are correlated to the forms of different groupings, such as friendship, comradeship, marriage, family, etc. Not only are these degrees related to such forms of communities, however, but according to Scheler, they are directly linked also to certain ethnological considerations. To lack of such basic considerations, current theories of our knowledge of the other partly owe their failure. Their claim to explain knowledge of others is not totally false; in believing that their theories were ultimate and absolute explanations, such men as Erdmann and Lipps were wrong, but from a relative point of view their theories have much to offer.

As we shall see, Scheler feels that the theories of analogy and of empathy are entirely based on the postulates of the psychology of association. The empathy theory of Lipps he sees as excellent for the study of "mass" psychology; and the theory of analogy certainly can be used justifiably to study modern man living in today's urbanized society (Gesellschaft). But as ultimate explanations of the problem of origins of social bonds these theories are incomplete.

4) The problem of empirical psychology. What contributions can empirical psychology make toward an explanation of our knowledge of other psychic centers? Scheler denies that it can furnish basic principles for a solution. For, empirical psychology already presupposes the fact of intersubjectivity and does not begin by establishing it. Empirical psychology presupposes that other men exist, and that we can know them as such; it presupposes the existence of psychic facts, perceptions, inner and outer experiences, feelings, etc.; it presupposes that all these psychic facts can be formulated in a judgment and can be communicated as intelligible to another; it presupposes that the other can understand this communication. "It is not for empirical psychology to provide an account of this understanding, sharing and reproduction of thought, for it is socially and epistemologically presupposed in its own procedure."[5]

Scheler faults empirical psychology especially for failing to realize the limits beyond which the psychical ceases to be objectifiable. Only a small part of the human being is an "object of knowledge," and of this part only a smaller part can be subjected to experimental tests. He notes that some experimentalists have claimed to study the higher psychic acts such as think-

[5] *Sympathy*, p. 222. "Nicht die empirische Psychologie kann dieses Verstehen dieses Mit- und Nachdenken klären: es ist eine sozialerkenntnis-theoretische Voraussetzung ihres Verfahrens." *Sympathie*, p. 239.

ing, willing, religious acts, etc., on the presupposition that *all* psychic and intellectual facts are accessible to experimental research. Scheler replies: "But to this it must be replied that the full significance of cognitive activity is not, and never can be accessible to internal awareness, or to apprehension, attention or observation, let alone to experimental interference; not by reason of any avoidable limitations of knowledge or method, but because of its intrinsic nature."[6] The realm of the *Person* and his spiritual acts is totally above the reach of experimental psychology which has only to do with the vital sphere. Only insofar as the acts of the *Person* require a resonance in the vital and psychic sphere are they accessible for observation. But no such observation, even if it be introspective, can open a door to the spiritual and intellectual life. "For this constitutes a whole region of being which lies entirely beyond the comprehension of empirical psychology, (experimental or otherwise), and this by virtue of its ontological status."[7]

Scheler holds on the contrary, that the spiritual *Person qua Person* represents a mode of being which is totally non-objectifiable and which is accessible to us only by means of intellectual or affective co-performance (*Mit-vollzug*) of the others spiritual "acts." In this way, we participate or "share" in the other's being (*Seinsteilnahme*). This sharing corresponds on the level of the non-objectifiable *Person* to the objective knowledge we have of non-personal things; and indeed, the latter knowledge is only a lesser form of participation. The *Person,* however, transcends the realm of such objectivity; his essence and its acts are therefore accessible only to "understanding." This constitutes a totally distinct source of facts. "Understanding therefore constitutes an ultimate source of facts and intuitive data at least on a level with 'awareness.'"[8]

Understanding, or comprehension, does not restrict itself to understanding others. The act of understanding is equally applicable to self. (In the case of others, we only understand them insofar as they permit us; this constitutes a great difference between knowledge of *Persons* and the world of nature.) Understanding, therefore, as the understanding of an act and its objective meaning is nothing other than the participation by one spiritual

[6] *Sympathy,* p. 223. "Dem gegenüber ist festzustellen, dass der gesamte Inbegriff der noetischen Akte nicht etwa vermöge prinzipiell verschiebbarer Wissens- und Methodengrenzen, sondern seinem ontischen Wesen gemäss weder innerlich 'wahrnehmbar,' noch bemerkbar, beachtbar und beobachtbar . . ." *Sympathie,* p. 239–40.

[7] *Sympathy,* p. 223. "Hier liegt ein ganzes Seinsgebiet, das vielmehr überhaupt empirischer Psychologie (sei sie experimentell oder nicht) *transintelligibel* ist, und dies auf Grund seines ontischen Wesens." *Sympathie,* p. 240.

[8] *Sympathy,* p. 224. "*Verstehen* ist also mindestens eine gleichursprüngliche originäre Quelle von Tatsachen und Anschauungsgegebenheiten wie 'Wahrnehmen.'" *Sympathie,* p. 241.

being in the life of another spiritual being, participation essentially different from perception and having nothing to do with it. This is why a phenomenology which seeks to know, through understanding them, concrete *Persons* and the concrete meaning of their intellectual, spiritual manifestations is totally different from a psychology which studies the objectifiable psychic reality; the difference is not only methodological, but substantial and essential.

But the *Person* as a spiritual being is not only non-objectifiable, he is also trans-intelligible, says Scheler. Unlike the world of dead matter, and the automatic sphere of the vital, the *Person* is free to reveal himself and make himself known or to refuse to do so. *Persons* can be silent, not in the sense of refusing to speak words, but also by a positive effort of concealment of attitudes and acts, for one can only know the other insofar as he wills to reveal himself through his acts. Of nature, including the sphere of the vital, we have a spontaneous knowledge; the object cannot act to conceal itself from us. The world of matter is inert before our inquisition; vital psychisms automatically and necessarily reveal themselves because of their psycho-somatic correlations. Only the spiritual *Person* can freely choose to open himself to be understood or to shut himself up from all comprehension by another.

In the light of this irreducible difference between the sphere of the spiritual *Person,* unique in his independence and trans-intelligibility, and the sphere of the vital-psychic, Scheler declares that empirical psychology can assist in the solution of the problem of intersubjectivity only within very narrow limits.

5) The metaphysical problem. There is an intimate connection between the solution one proposes for the problem of intersubjectivity and the metaphysics on which such a solution rests. Scheler finds, for example that the theory of inference or analogy is based upon the metaphysical assumption of the cartesian system of two separate substances inter-acting one upon the other. Any solution proposed, therefore, will ultimately justify itself by the metaphysical system underlying it.

6) The problem of values. There have been theories of intersubjectivity which approached the problem from the ethico-juridical point of view. They have sought to justify the existence of other human beings on the presence of the moral imperative and the sense of obligation inherent in man. Of these attempts, that of Fichte is perhaps the most completely elaborated. According to him there exists a primary consciousness of obligation, which forms the very essence of the Ego; this requires that there be other Egos exterior to me toward whom I have obligations. All theoretical knowledge of the

existence of exterior Egos, depends therefore for Fichte, on the practical evidence of my consciousness of obligation and is completely independent of any theoretical affirmation.

Scheler rejects as unsatisfactory, this attempt to establish the independent existence of the other, although he admits that the general direction from which the approach is made has a certain validity. The moral conscience as such and by itself constitutes an "indirect guarantee" of the existence of other persons, but in no way a direct or primary evidence either of the existence of other persons or their possible value. We shall see later that Scheler realizes the important results which may be obtained from a phenomenological analysis of moral social acts as proof for his theory of the general sociality of man. He does not, however, invoke this in his specific theory of the knowledge of individual persons. This leads him to make the distinction which we have previously seen in the first problem he posed above, namely the problem of the social a priori of man in general. This question must be clearly distinguished from the particular instance of this man's knowledge of that man. It is with the latter that any theory of intersubjectivity must especially deal.

Scheler's survey of the problems involved in the knowledge of other individuals is a very complete one. He has, as he had promised, analysed the whole into a number of sub-problems and thus helped to reduce the confusion which has always been associated with the study of man's relationship with others. Whether Scheler's attempt to solve the difficulties raised is successful or not, he must be credited with having put the discussion on a sounder basis.

However clearly Scheler may have seen the whole problem, we must admit that unfortunately his own solution is not commendable for its freedom from obscurity. His approach to the problem has been determined by his metaphysics of the *Person,* and specifically by his separation of the human individual into two psychic levels, that of "*Person*" and that of Ego. The necessity for distinguishing a spiritual psychic center in man has never been denied by classical philosophy, but with Scheler the distinction becomes so great that it amount to a *separation* of two aspects in man which now admit of only a dynamic interrelation. The metaphysics of the individual human being, which had emerged from Scheler's ethical studies and had been crystallized in the "*Person-Ich*" theory, begins to show fatal weaknesses when Scheler attempts to account for the phenomena of intersubjectivity.

As we have seen above, Scheler insisted in his ethical work that the *Person* and his specifically personal "acts" could never become "objects" of knowledge, either for the self or for another self. Knowledge of our "acts" was possible only by a simultaneous comprehension or reflection in which they were not reduced to the status of "objects." As Schuetz has pointed out, the denial of the possibility of such reflective knowledge "involves, of course, the abandonment of a basic principle of phenomenology, namely, that any kind of experience can be grasped by a reflective act."[9] Why Scheler ruled out such knowledge is not made clear. It is all the more puzzling when we note how much the founder of phenomenology, Husserl, had insisted on it. The *Person-Ich* distinction emerges again in the theory of intersubjectivity proposed by Scheler. For this reason his theory divides naturally into two parts, one concerned with the perception of the other Ego, (*Wahrnehmungs-theorie des fremden Ich*), and the second concerned with the understanding of the other's "acts."

Since for Scheler neither the acts nor their source, the *Person*, can be made "objects" for knowledge, there does not arise for him the necessity of explaining how we "perceive" the *Person*. The *Person* is not perceived, but "understood," "comprehended," by simultaneous co-performance of the acts of the other. This, however, does not take place separately from the perception of the other Ego, for in Scheler's view, the physical and psychical sides of man are always presented as a totality and grasped as such.[10]

After exploring the entire problem of intersubjectivity, in the six questions given above, Scheler structures his own analysis by two broad questions: 1) do we have a knowledge of the existence of other men "in general?" 2) do we have knowledge of particular individuals, and how is this possible?

Scheler answers the first of these questions by his general theory of the social a priori which we shall discuss briefly. The second question divides naturally into two parts: a) how do we perceive the lower psychic center, Ego, of the other? b) how do we know the higher spiritual center, *Person*, of the other? Scheler's answer to this latter question as we have already

[9] Alfred Schuetz, "Scheler's Theory of Intersubjectivity and the General Thesis of the Alter Ego," *Philosophy and Phenomenological Research*, 2 (1941–2), p. 340, note.

[10] Scheler's insistence that the other *Person* is not an object, but is reached by an understanding that involves a co-performance of his acts simultaneous with a perception of the expressive dimension of his bodily features should be viewed in the light of the shift in German psychological theory that occured during his lifetime; against the old theory of associationism which emphasized an analytic study of elements, the new psychologists stressed that the subject for psychology was rather the total individual in whom alone the elements were intelligible. The "personalistic psychology" of William Stern, the various forms of *Verstehendenpsychologie* and *Gestalt* psychology are all witness to this shift in emphasis. Cf. William Stern, *General Psychology from the Personalistic Standpoint*, New York, Macmillan, 1938.

seen, is given in his theory of "understanding" the other person by co-performing (*Mitvollzug*) his spiritual acts. This solution was already determined by Scheler's denial of the possibility of objectification of spirit or its acts. Consequently Scheler offers no elaborate theory of the possibility and the conditions of understanding the spiritual *Person*. Since, however, the lower psychic center, the Ego, is always an object for knowledge, Scheler develops an involved theory to account for the possibility of its perception.

We shall proceed, therefore, after noting briefly Scheler's theory of the social a priori, to examine his critique of previous solutions to the problem of intersubjectivity. In the next chapter Scheler's own theory will be presented.

Knowledge of the Other in General

There are two key points that underlie Scheler's analysis of the intersubjective situation. He insists, first, that the bonds of community between men are states-of-affairs that are as real and objective as physical facts. Furthermore, this independently existing world of social facts is not arrived at by an additive, piecemeal process, but it is given first as a whole frame of reference within which individual relationships are rendered intelligible. For Scheler the social dimension of man's being is an a priori equally as essential as his intellectual or volitive dimensions. "What we are saying (in our own terminology), is simply that the world of the Thou, or the community, is just as much an *independent sphere of essential being* as are the spheres of the external world, the internal world, the bodily environment and the realm of the divine. But *every* truly irreducible sphere of being must necessarily be given as a whole *beforehand,* as a 'background' to the positing of the reality of any possible object within it; hence it does not simply comprise the sum of all the contingent facts within it."[11]

In his discussion of a social a priori in man in connection with his ethical study, Scheler had posed the question whether an individual who had never in his whole life encountered another man, nor perceived the slightest trace or sign indicating the existence of a being equally human, whether such a man could arrive at the notion of the existence of society and of other

[11] *Sympathy,* p. 236. "Wir sagen (in unserer Terminologie) nichts Anderes, als dass die Duwelt oder die Gemeinschaftswelt genau so eine *selbständige Wesensphäre* des Seienden ist wie die Aussenweltsphäre, die Innenweltsphäre, die Leib-Umweltsphäre die Sphäre des Göttlichen. Für *jede* echte unreduzible 'Sphäre' des Seienden gilt aber, dass sie als Wesensganzheit der Realsetzung jedes möglichen Gegenstandes in ihr als 'Hintergrund' *vorgegeben* ist; dass sie also keineswegs nur die Summe aller zufälligen Fakta in ihr bildet." *Sympathie,* p. 254.

intellectual-psychic beings. Would such a "Robinson Crusoe" (as Scheler calls him) realize that he himself belonged to a community of men?

Scheler answers both questions in the affirmative. Such a man he declares would be able to say: "I know that human communities exist and that I belong to one or many of them, but I do not know either the individuals who compose them or the type of groups into which *de facto* communities are divided." This clearly reveals the distinction, which Scheler insists upon, between knowledge of the *fact* of other human beings and knowledge of any *particular member* of the human community.

On what evidence, therefore, would such a priori knowledge be possible? It would be based on evidence which Scheler takes as intuitively certain, specifically on an occasionally experienced "awareness of absence" (*Leerbewusstsein*) stemming from the non-presence of another human being capable of becoming object of certain emotional acts which by their nature are destined to reach other human beings and which, failing in this, generate a definite experience of incompleteness in the individual. In other words, such a Crusoe would experience a feeling of emptiness and non-satisfaction every time he wished to execute those acts of an intellectual and psychic nature which have an *objective meaning* only if there exists another person to whom they are directed or from whom they require a response. Such an experience of frustration would be sufficient to give an intuition and a very positive idea of the sphere of the other. The idea of a human community in general would not, therefore, be in any way an "innate" idea, nor one transcending experience. On the contrary, it would be based upon the most intense and personal experience.

Any analysis of the "essentially social acts" (*Wesenssoziale Akte*) indicates that by their very nature they refer to the existing other person. Without the existence of others such acts would be meaningless and incomprehensible. Such, for example, are acts of love, responsibility, duty, gratitude. While Scheler does not hold with that school of thought claiming to derive the existence of others and society purely from an analysis of the concept of a moral being, as Fichte for example attempted, he sees that this approach contains a grain of truth: "There is one point in which this theory is quite correct: namely that pure value-relationships and the corresponding evaluative ties between persons do engender *unique* (i.e. autonomous) *sources of emotional evidence* independent of (theoretical) grounds for existence, *in favor of the value* (and hence the existence) of other persons and personal communities."[12] In other words, it would cer-

[12] *Sympathy*, p. 229. "Eines an dieser Theorie ganz richtig: Dass nämlich aus den puren Wertverhältnissen und ihnen entsprechenden Wertverhaltungsbeziehungen zwi-

tainly be erroneous to say that a being who was incapable of theoretic, objective knowledge, but capable of loving, hating, willing, possessed no evidence of the existence of other persons. We may say, therefore, that "taken by itself indeed, the moral consciousness offers a 'guarantee' that is not direct, let alone primary, but *indirect,* not only for the possibility of value, but also for the existence of other people."[13]

Not "moral consciousness" in the abstract, but specific concrete acts experienced by the individual lead Scheler to the conclusion that man is always conscious of living *in* community with others. He insists on the uniqueness of all "social acts" as intentional in an a priori sense:

> Nor does this apply to some one moral act or another, but to all morally relevant acts, experiences and states, in so far as they contain an intentional reference to other moral persons; obligation, merit, gratitude and so on, all refer, by the very nature of the acts themselves, to other people, without implying that such persons must already have been encountered in some sort of experience, and above all without warranting the assumption that these intrinsically social acts (as we shall call them), can only have occurred and originated in the actual commerce of men with one another.[14]

It is sufficient, declares Scheler, to examine these acts and experiences to prove that it is impossible to reduce them to a combination of simple "presocial" acts and experiences to which has been added the accidental experience of meeting other men. These acts show, that given the essential structure of the human consciousness, society exists, so to speak, in the interior of each individual, that if man constitutes part of society, society in its turn, constitutes part of man, to whom it is bound by these essential relations. Therefore, if the "I" is a constitutive element of the "we," the "we" is a constitutive element no less necessary of the "I."

schen Personen eigene (d.i. autonome) und von den (theoretischen) Seinsgründen *unabhängige emotionale Wissensevidenzen für das Wertsein* (und darum auch für das Dasein) fremder Personen und Gemeinschaften solcher gewachsen." *Sympathie,* p. 246.

[13] *Sympathy,* p. 229. "das sittliche Bewusstsein für sich allein ist in der Tat eine *indirekte,* nicht aber eine direkte, geschweige gar eine primäre 'Gewähr' nicht nur für mögliches Wertsein, sondern auch für das Dasein fremder Personen." *Sympathie,* p. 247.

[14] *Sympathy,* p. 229. "Nicht nur dieser oder jener sittliche Akt, sondern alle sittlich relevanten Akte, Erlebnisse und Zustände – soweit in ihnen die Wesensbeziehung auf andere sittliche Personwesen intentional eingeschlossen ist (Schuld, Verdienst, Verantwortung, Pflichtbewusstsein, Liebe, Versprechen, Dank, usw.) – weisen in der Tat schon von sich aus kraft ihrer Aktnatur auf fremde Personwesen hin, ohne dass darum diese fremden Personen schon in der zufälligen Erfahrung mussten vorher gegeben sein; ohne dass man vor allem zur Annahme berechtigt wäre, es seien diese Akte – wir nennen sie wesenssoziale Akte – erst in tatsächlichem Verkehr des Menschen mit dem Menschen entsprungen und entstanden." *Sympathie,* p. 247.

Furthermore, says Scheler, one can even ask if the existence of these essential relations by which each individual and particular "I" is attached to every possible human collectivity does not form a primitive fact, in the sense that a purely immanent examination of the essential manifestations of the activities of each "I," an examination which would be anterior to all accidental empirical knowledge and independent as well from all real interaction of men, if such an examination would not enable us to discover in man a tendency to integration in a great number of substantially different groups, a tendency to adhere to a great number of values common to these groups.

Man, therefore, says Scheler, at least as regards his spiritual center, is ordered in an a priori fashion to other human beings to such a degree that even in the absence of any empirical meeting with other men he would be aware of his social nature. Nor would it be necessary, Scheler adds, that man perceive the expressive movements of the body of the other in order to arrive at the particular knowledge of the existence of another spiritual *Person*. "But I cannot concede it for the assumption that spiritual *Persons* exist, since this assumption . . . only requires a rational content of meaning in *some* sort of objective sign-material – and by no means necessarily involves that the body should be present."[15] This of course, does not mean that Scheler belittles the importance of the role which perception of the other's bodily expression plays in our knowledge of other people. As we shall see, he accords a paramount place to the factor of expression. What he insists, however, is that even prior to the perception of another human being, one *could* arrive at a knowledge of the general fact that such an intellectual being *did exist*. The further step, knowledge of a specific individual requires of course that the other be actually present. It then becomes possible for the *Person,* the highest spiritual center in man, to "understand" the other not by making the latter's *Person* an "object" of knowledge, but by co-performing the spiritual acts of the other.

Scheler's insistence on the fact of the social a priori in general, cogent though his arguments may be, does not settle the problem which he has set out to solve. It is not the fact that "in general" we know of the existence of other men which is the central problem; the point at which disagreement begins is when we attempt to explain how we know the individual other, understanding "know" in the broadest sense as covering acts of knowledge,

[15] *Sympathie*, p. 236. "Nicht vermag ich es zuzugeben für die Annahme der Existenz geistiger Personen, deren Annahme . . . nur vernünftige Sinngehalte in *irgendwelchem* objektivem Zeichenmaterial voraussetzt – keineswegs notwendig Leibgegebenheit." *Sympathie*, p. 254.

of participation, and of sharing in the psychic acts and affections of the other.

On the basis of the metaphysics of the *Person* which Scheler erected, specifically, on the basis of his distinction – and near separation – of the two psychic centers in man, the *Person* and the Ego, he had to satisfy a double necessity, to explain how each center of man is correlated to the corresponding center in the other. This involved him in a two-fold problem concerning knowledge of the other, that of "understanding" and that of "perception."

Scheler actually has no "theory" explaining how "understanding" makes possible the intersubjective relations between *Persons*. He asserts the fact without giving phenomenological justification. For, as we have indicated above, he offers no elaboration of exactly how it is possible to "co-perform" the acts of the other *Person*. He rather sees it as flowing from the very essence of Spirit (*Geist*) that such participation or sharing of spiritual acts can take place. As a result his phenomenology of intersubjectivity concentrates almost entirely on the problem of how one Ego can relate to another Ego. Since we have already explained what little Scheler has to say about the relationships between *Persons* effected through the co-performance of acts, we shall discuss now only the explanation he provides for the possibility of intersubjectivity through the perception of the other Ego. Before setting forth his own theory, however, he felt it necessary to refute the two classical theories which had been accepted regarding the perception of the other. A brief survey of his refutation will show us the particular point of view from which Scheler approached the problem.

Two Classical Theories

The difficulties which encumber the problem of our perception of the other all stem, says Scheler, from the initial, but gratuitous assumption, that what is first "given" to each one is his own self and his own psychic experiences, certain of which experiences refer to other individuals. When the problem is approached from this assumption two questions immediately arise: 1) how can we distinguish those psychic experiences which relate to others from those which concern ourselves; 2) what evidence for the existence of the other do our psychic experiences about the other carry with them?

Previous investigation into the perception of the other has been based on this initial assumption of the priority of the knowledge of self. Scheler intends to show that the failure to solve the problem satisfactorily is traceable to this basic premise. He therefore examines the two major theories which have been advanced to solve the problem from this direction and proves that neither theory can justify itself. He concludes therefore that the initial assumption is unwarranted, and sets forth as his own starting point a thesis which will not accord to self-knowledge such priority as had been previously granted. In the full explanation of his counter-theory of simultaneity, however, he resorts to a somewhat bizarre assumption of an original undifferentiated psychic field, shared by all Egos, the existence of which he feels forced to postulate to account for certain phenomena encountered in his analysis of the forms of sympathy.

The two theories which Scheler declares have been based on the assumption of the priority of self-knowledge are the two classical ones in the psychology of personality. The first is that of analogy or inference (*Analogieschluss*); the second is the theory of empathy (*Einfühlungstheorie*).

The theory of analogy states that we base our conviction of the existence of other psychic centers, exterior to us but similar to ourselves, upon the perception in the other organism of movements analogous to our own activity.

The theory of empathy is based on the hypothesis that we believe in the existence of other psychic centers similar to our own because of an empathetic projection of our "Ego-ness" into a body exterior to our own.

Scheler offers two criticism of each of these theories: a) neither one is internally warranted by experience; b) the difficulties in each can be traced to their initial assumption of the priority of self-knowledge.

Against the theory of analogy Scheler poses four arguments: 1) As Hume had said and as Koehler has demonstrated, even animals are aware of the existence of other psychic centers, and they could never have arrived at this knowledge by inference. Furthermore, the work of child psychologists such as William Stern indicates that the infant has a definite knowledge of other persons at an age when no one could possibly attribute this to the power of inference.

2) We are certainly conscious of our own expressions, but we do not "see" our gestures in the same fashion as we see the movements of others. Prescinding from the instance of reflection in mirrors, etc., our own bodily movements are known to us by kinesthetic sensations, whereas the gestures and expressions of the other are given to us within the visual field of perception. Between such visual phenomena and our own kinesthetic sensations, there is no common ground for an inference or analogy establishing the existence of another psychic center. Only after we have previously arrived at the existence of another psychic center can we proceed to make

judgments of analogy based on his expressive gestures. The fact that we take gestures as "expressions" already presupposes that we have reached the existence of another psychism.

3) Furthermore, says Scheler, we consider that animals like birds and fish possess a type of psychic life, yet their expressive actions in no way resemble ours.

4) Finally, the theory of analogy introduces into its argument the fallacy of the fourth term. The logical conclusion of the argument should be, not that there are other beings similar to me, but that I find exterior to me, exact replicas of myself: "For such an argument would be logically correct (and not a fallacy of four terms) only if it implied that on the occurrence of expressive movements similar to those I perform myself, *it is my own self that is present here as well – and not some other and alien self.* If the conclusion refers to an alien self distinct from my own, it is a false conclusion, an instance of the fallacy of four terms."[16]

The second well known theory, that of empathy, is also refuted by Scheler, who says that even in its most complete formulation, as given by Theodore Lipps, it is a mere hypothesis incapable of justification. Scheler does not deny the fact of empathy; on the contrary, his investigations on this have been very extensive. What he does deny, however, it that by means of empathy we first come to a knowledge of the existence of other exterior psychic centers. Empathy, by its very nature, presupposes that the existence of the other has already been given. "For it would be pure chance that the process of empathy should coincide with the actual presence of mind in the bodies so perceived."[17]

Other difficulties encumber the theory. On the basis of it, it would be impossible to distinguish the difference which exists between the case in which we empathetically impute life to a being actually lacking it (in the animism of primitives for instance) and the case in which life is genuinely present. Again, this theory does not admit a sufficiently clear distinction between real affective fusion as a source of knowledge of the other psychism, and affective fusion or empathy of a purely aesthetic kind, as when we unite ourselves by empathy to Hamlet played on the stage by an actor.

[16] *Sympathy,* p. 240–21. "Denn logisch richtig (und keine *quarternio terminorum*) wäre ja der Analogieschluss nur dann, wenn, er dahin lautete, dass, wenn gleiche Ausdrucksbewegungen da sind, wie ich sie vollziehe, auch *mein Ich hier noch einmal vorhanden sei – nicht aber ein fremdes und anderes Ich.* Soll der Schluss ein fremdes, von meinem Ich verschiedenes Ich setzen, so ist er ein falscher Schluss, eine quarternio terminorum." *Sympathie,* p. 259.

[17] *Sympathy,* p. 241. "Denn dass nun der Prozess der Einfühlung mit wirklicher Beseelung der Körper, in die wir 'einfühlen,' zusammenträfe, das wäre hier ein purer 'Zufall.'" *Sympathie,* p. 259.

On the basis of what "given" would empathy be possible, asks Scheler. Would it suffice that certain perceptions in the visual field be given us? Unquestionably not, since there are many objects given by visual perception which never become objects of empathy for us. It has been said by defenders of the theory that for empathy there is required the visual perception of "expressive movements." Scheler correctly objects that this begs the question. "For the realization that certain seen movements represent expressive movements already presupposes knowledge of the presence of another mind of some kind."[18] The fact that we conceive certain movements as expressive movements, far from being a foundation for our knowledge that another psychism exists, rather is a consequence of such knowledge. Indeed, on the very principles of the theory of empathy such an explanation is excluded, for according to it, other animated beings exist only following empathy. There would be required, therefore, a double fusion: a fusion of our own feeling of life with certain sensible complexes, and a fusion of the Ego with the complex thus animated. This merely removes the difficulty one step further, for the question still recurs: what is the objectively "given" which justifies our projection of life into such complexes of sensations?

In a word, the theory of projective empathy cannot explain the hypothesis by which it would postulate the existence of the other Ego exterior to myself. It could furnish a support to my belief that I rediscover *my* Ego elsewhere, but would not reveal *another* Ego distinct from my own. We are ordinarily convinced, however, both that there exist other Egos exterior to us and distinct from our own Ego, and also that we can know, though incompletely, their particular and characteristically individual essences. And for Scheler, we could come to a knowledge of the existence in general of other individuals without any perception of another's physical body. Discovery of signs or traces of distinctly spiritual activity would suffice. "For wherever we meet with *signs* or *traces* of its spiritual activity, in a work of art, for instance, or in the felt unity of a voluntary action, we immediately encounter in this an active individual self."[19]

What the theory of empathy cannot explain is that all modifications of expressive behavior are comprehensible only on condition that we have prior knowledge of the individual unity behind them. According to Scheler,

[18] *Sympathy,* p. 241. "Dass die optischen Bilder irgendwelcher Bewegungen Bilder von Ausdrucksbewegungen sind, das ist eine Einsicht, welche die Kenntnis des Bestandes eines fremden beseelten Etwas eben bereits voraussetzt." *Sympathie,* p. 260.

[19] *Sympathy,* p. 242. "Auch wo uns irgendwelche *Zeichen* und *Spuren* seiner geistigen Tätigleit gegeben sind, wie z.B. ein Kunstwerk oder die fühlbare Einheit eines willentlichen Wirkens, erfassen wir hierin ohne weiteres ein tätiges individuelles Ich." *Sympathie,* p. 261.

bodily expressions and psychic experiences have *in themselves* nothing which would permit me to assign them to one individual center rather than another. Only because I understand them through the unity of the individual *Person* can I determine them to their proper center. "I experience my body as mine (and the body of another as belonging to someone else), because I know that both self and body (in its mental and physical aspects) belong to one and the same concrete individual *Person.* Both self and body acquire their ultimate individual character from their evident connection with the unitary *Person.*"[20]

Therefore, for Scheler, it is not the *content* of consciousness which determines the individualization of the Ego. Identical psychic facts, such as they would appear to an ideally perfect internal perception, could belong to different individual Egos. But a psychic "individual" is never a simple totality, a simple "sum" of psychic experiences, or a synthesis of these experiences. Rather every psychic fact is concrete only because I apprehend in it at the same time an individual, or because it becomes for me the symbol announcing the existence of this individual. This is why what we first apprehend of the other are not merely isolated facts, but always and primarily the totality of the psychic character of that individual being in his whole expression. To account for this neither the analogy theory nor the theory of projective empathy is adequate.

[20] *Sympathy*, p. 243. "Ich erlebe meinen Körper als meinen (und auch den fremden Körper als zu einem Anderen gehörig), da es dieselbe konkrete einheitliche Person ist, der ich Beides, das Ich und den Leib (als Seelen und Körperleib), zugehörig weiss. Sowohl das Ich wie der Leib findet in der erlebharen Zugehörigkeit zur einheitlichen *Person* seine letzte Individualisierung." *Sympathie*, p. 262.

CHAPTER V

SCHELER'S THEORY OF INTERSUBJECTIVITY

We have outlined in the last chapter Scheler's refutation of the two classical theories which have been advanced to explain our knowledge of other psychic centers. His criticism as such is internal; it proves that neither theory can explain the facts without involving itself in contradictions. He has, however, a more fundamental criticism to offer, one by which he simultaneously presents his own theory of intersubjectivity at the Ego level.

As we have already mentioned, Scheler attributes the failure of the two classical theories to their two initial assumptions: 1) that we know first our own psychic experiences, certain of which we later distinguish as referring to others; 2) that what is first given to us in knowledge of the other is only the appearance of his physical body; from the movements and alterations of the physical body we then presumably can postulate the existence of another Ego exterior to ourselves.

Scheler analyzes these two assumptions to see if they are justified. The defenders of them have often denied the necessity for justification on the grounds that they were both "self-evident truths" (*selbstverständlich*). Can we, they ask, think any thoughts but our own, experience any feelings but our own? Again, what else could we possibly be given primarily in our knowledge of the other except the appearance of his physical body, to which is due the physical emanations necessary for any perception?

"Self-evident" propositions must always submit to reexamination, says Scheler, especially when they claim to express the limits of what can and can not be given in experience. He therefore tests these propositions by a reexamination of the given data. The result of his analysis leads him to deny both assumptions and set up in their place two basic principles of his own. 1) Against the assumption of the priority of self-knowledge he sets forth his theory of the common psychic field. 2) He declares that the other is first given to us not as mere bodily appearance, but as a physical-psychical totality; and consequently that the psychic facts as revealed through "expression" are perceived simultaneously with the physical.

The Original Psychic Field

The assumption of the priority of self-knowledge is based upon the belief that internal perception or intuition (*Wahrnehmung oder Anschauung*), which alone can yield knowledge of the psychic, is restricted to *self*-perception. It has been accepted as self-evident "that it is our *own* individual self and its experiences which are 'immediately given' in that mode of intuition, by which alone the mental, a self and its experiences, can possibly be apprehended, namely in inner intuition and perception."[1] What phenomenological proof can be presented for this assertion, Scheler asks.

The usual statement that "each can only think his own thoughts, feel his own feelings," is no "self-evident" truth. On the contrary, he declares, the only self-evident thing here is the fact that as soon as I presuppose a real substratum for the experiences which I have, then all the thoughts and feelings which "I" think and feel belong to this substratum. This is a mere tautological assertion, he declares. It is obvious that two real substrata, two psychic substances, or two brains, can in no way merge one into another. We must leave aside such tautologies and conduct the investigation along strict phenomenological lines. As soon as this is done, the "self-evident" nature of the proposition disappears, for nothing is more certain than the fact that we can think the thoughts of another as well as our own, can experience through sympathy (*Mitfühlen*) the feelings of another as well as our own. Do we not presuppose this in daily life, asks Scheler. Do we not constantly make the distinction between "our" thoughts and those which another shares with us; between "our" feelings and those which we experience by affective reproduction (*Nachfühlen*) or affective contagion (*Gefühlsansteckung*); between "our" will and that which is imposed on us, either in a normal or even in a hypnotic state?

There are four possibilities which Scheler mentions in this assignment of thoughts and feelings to the proper Ego. 1) Our thoughts can be given us as ours and the thoughts of another as his; this happens in simple communication. 2) The thoughts of another can be given not as his, but as ours; such would be the situation in the case of remembering things heard or read, or in the case where we assimilate the thoughts of parents or teachers without afterwards consciously referring these to their true source. 3) Again we may project our own thoughts into another without fully realizing the extent of

[1] *Sympathy,* p. 244. "Dass es das *eigene* Ichindividuum und seine Erlebnisse sind, die in der Anschauungsrichtung, durch die wesenhaft überhaupt nur Psychisches, ein Ich und seins Erlebnisse zu erfassen sind, nämlich in der Richtung der 'inneren' Anschauung oder Wahrnehmung, 'zunächst' gegeben sind." *Sympathie,* p. 263.

this; the Christian interpreters of Aristotle, for example, did this constantly. 4) Finally, says Scheler, a psychic experience may present itself which is not readily assignable either to myself or to the other. It is with this last case that Scheler is concerned.

The first three stages have shown, he says, that the same psychic experiences may be given both "as ours" and "as the other's." It may equally happen that an experience be simply given without any characteristic mark of "mine" or "thine." "It is possible, therefore . . . for the same experiences to be given both 'as our own' *and* 'as someone else's'; but there is also the case in which an experience is simply given, *without presenting itself either as our own or as another's,* as invariably happens, for example, where we are in doubt as to which of the two it is."[2]

This fourth stage is the absolutely primary one; within it the differentiation of psychic experiences and the correct assignment of them to the separate individual psychic centers has not yet taken place. This stage of sheer psychic "givenness" provides the common starting point for the development of the gradual, increasingly determined assignment of experience to the "self" and the "other;" there is a concentration of the Ego and its experiences accompanied by a simultaneous withdrawal from the other.

The older theories had proposed that we reached the other by assigning certain of our own primarily given psychic experiences to the corporeal phenomena of the other. Scheler advances in opposition his theory of the originally undifferentiated field of the psychic, of an amorphous stream of experience out from which the individual psychic centers gradually emerge. We have thus "an immediate flow of experiences, *undifferentiated as between mine and thine,* which actually contains both our own and others' experiences intermingled and without distinction from one another. Within this flow there is a gradual formation of ever more stable vortices, which slowly attract further elements of the stream into their orbits and thereby become successively and very gradually identified with distinct individuals."[3]

[2] *Sympathy,* p. 246. "Können aber . . . dieselben Erlebnisse 'als unsere' *und* 'als die Anderer' gegeben sein, so gibt es auch den Fall, dass ein Erlebnis einfach 'gegeben' ist, *ohne noch sei es als eigenes oder fremdes gegeben zu sein* – wie es z.B. immer da zunächst ist, wo wir zweifeln, ob das Eine oder das Andere der Fall ist." *Sympathie,* p. 265.

[3] *Sympathy,* p. 246. ". . . ein *in Hinsicht auf Ich-Du indifferenter Strom der Erlebnisse* fliesst 'zunächst' dahin, der faktisch Eigenes und Fremdes ungeschieden und ineinandergemischt enthält; und in diesem Strome bilden sich erst allmählich fester gestaltete Wirbel, die langsam immer neue Elemente des Stromes in ihre Kreise ziehen und in diesem Prozesse sukzessive und sehr allmählich verschiedenen Individuen zugeordnet werden." *Sympathie,* p. 265–6.

This original "stream" of psychic experience is not given to us totally unrelated to the different psychic centers which it contains. Rather, according to Scheler, all given experience is related to an ego in a general sense, ("Ein Ich uberhaupt"); what is not determined for us at this stage is, he insists, the definite fact of knowing *to which* particular Ego, mine or another's, the given experience pertains. For, "which individual self it may be, that owns a given experience, whether it is our own or another's, is something that is not necessarily apparent in the experience as immediately presented."[4]

The thesis of the originally undifferentiated psychic stream is of major importance in Scheler's theory of intersubjectivity. It enables him to do away with the necessity of explaining by analogy or empathy the power of one self to reach the knowledge of another's psychic life. Knowledge of the other is not only concomitant with, but in a sense, even prior to self-knowledge, for reflective self-knowledge emerges later. Man begins life completely integrated in a life community (*Gemeinschaft*) and only gradually marks off more and more clearly the boundaries of the self. His knowledge of the psychic experience of others begins at a time when he cannot distinguish his own from another's experience.

The solution proposed by Scheler, is, to say the least, radical. Whereas previous attempts had always seen the Ego starting from self-consciousness and advancing toward a gradual awareness of others, Scheler's theory places the whole problem on a totally different basis. He reverses the entire situation. Consciousness of others is prior to self-consciousness, and only out from the whole stream of experienced psychic life does the individual gradually come to *self*-consciousness whereby he correctly refers psychic experience to himself and to others. As a consequence Scheler has avoided the problem which earlier investigations had faced in attempting to introduce a knowledge of others only after self-realization had been reached. Man is primarily and unavoidable social. "A man tends, in the first instance, to live more in *others* than in himself; more in the community than in his own individual self."[5]

As further proof of his remarkable theory of the priority of the social factor in the rise of consciousness Scheler adduces two instances. The scientific study of child psychology and the psychology of primitives suffice to

[4] *Sympathy*, p. 246. "... welches Ichindividuum es sei, zu dem ein 'erlebtes' Erlebnis gehört, ob es unser eigenes oder ein fremdes ist, das ist in der primären Gegebenheit der Erlebnisse nicht notwendig mitgegeben." *Sympathie*, p. 266.

[5] *Sympathy*, p. 247. "Zunächst lebt der Mensch mehr in den *Anderen* als in sich selbst; mehr in der Gemeinschaft als in seinem Individuum." *Sympathie*, p. 266.

establish the fact, he declares. From the beginning the child is immersed in the family "spirit," he lives without that degree of self-consciousness that would distinguish physical and psychical, interior and exterior, material objects and living subjects, his own thoughts and ideas from those of others. The line between self and environment is not yet established; initially the entire field of phenomena is taken as a vast animated whole in which the self is not distinguished off from other psychic entities. Only very slowly does the child "raise his own spiritual head" (erhebt es sein eignes geistiges Haupt) above the enveloping stream of common psychic experience and begin to mark off the boundaries of self-experience and that of others. By a process of objectification he establishes a distance between some of the psychic experiences which are present to him and locates them within other psychic centers in the general field. Thus, by the time the child reaches the point at which the distinction between self-experience and the experiences of others is clearly made, he has already been living in a psychic union with others for a long time.

No distinct problem therefore presents itself, on Scheler's theory, as regards the possibility of one psychic center establishing contact with another in a direct, non-inferential, non-analogous way. The process is rather the reverse. From an initial situation in which the self is too diffused to permit of the objectification of others, we pass to the concretizing, solidifying position effected by a withdrawal from others to a point at which the self becomes conscious of itself as complete-in-itself; this position, however, does not break the lines of communication between self and others, but only lengthens them, and in this way distinguishes and objectifies the centers of communication involved. By the time the adult stage is reached the self is an independent, fully *self*-consciousness psychism; the fact, however that reflective self-consciousness has so evolved does not deny access to other psychic centers but only enables one to determine when "another" and his experiences enter the conscious field.

The results of research among primitive peoples lead us to the same conclusion according to Scheler. He takes the phenomena which have been encountered by such investigators as Levy-Bruhl to indicate a real fusion of the individual with the soul of the community. "A similar immersion in the spirit of the community and conformity to the shapes and patterns of its flow, can also be seen in all primitive peoples."[6] For example, the impulse toward vengeance which impels the members of a tribe or family to seek out

[6] *Sympathy,* p. 248. "Eben die Eingeschmolzenheit in die Seele der Gemeinschaft und in die Schemata und Formen dieser Strömung zeigt auch alles primitive Menschentum." *Sympathie,* p. 267.

the one who has offended any member stems not from sympathy which would correctly imply injury to "another," but rather it derives from an identification of the individuals with the community.

The Area of "Inner Perception"

Scheler's substitution of the originally undifferentiated psychic field in place of the older theory of the priority of self-knowledge immediately raises a difficulty, as he himself clearly sees: "But how then is it possible to observe the mental life of another person? Let us now go on from the phenomenological fact that a mental experience may be presented in 'internal perception' *regardless* of whether it is 'my' experiences or (characteristically) someone else's, to the question how such a thing is possible. For is not 'internal perception' necessarily also a perception of *oneself*? Is it possible to have internal perception of another self and the inner life of *another* person?" [7] The reply to this difficulty naturally turns on the precise meaning of "inner perception." Scheler feels that there has been great confusion on this point and he attempts to clear it up by distinguishing the proper areas of inner and outer experience.

He admits that previous philosophers have held that inner intuition or perception yields only self-experience. "But 'internal intuition' can certainly not be defined by reference to its object, by saying that a person engaged in such intuition is perceiving 'himself.'" [8] For once we say that the intuited inner experience is always self-experience, then perception of the psychic life of the other would be by definition impossible, since only inner intuition can grasp objects in the psychic sphere. The term "inner," therefore, indicates for Scheler, only the direction, and not the object of the perception. It is clear that I can know myself equally by outer perception through the visual or tactile sense. Now, just as outer perception is not limited to my knowledge of others, neither is inner perception limited to my knowledge of my own psychic acts. Inner perception rather indicates the faculty of the psychic in general whose area is the whole psychic field. "Thus internal

[7] *Sympathy,* p. 248. "Wie ist nun aber Wahrnehmung fremden Seelenlebens möglich? Wenden wir uns von dieser phanomenologischen Feststellung, dass ein psychisches Erleben durch 'innere Wahrnehmung' gegeben sein kann noch *indifferent,* ob es 'mein' Erleben oder (im Sosein) das eines Anderen ist, nun zu der Frage, wie solches möglich sei. Ist denn 'innere Wahrnehmung' nicht auch eo ipso 'Selbstwahrnehmung?' Ist es möglich, das Ich und Erleben eines Anderen innerlich 'wahrzunehmen?'" *Sympathie,* p. 268.

[8] *Sympathy,* p. 249. "Innere Anschauung ist aber durchaus nicht durch die Objektbestimmung definiert, dass der so innerlich Anschauende 'sich selbst' wahrnahme." *Sympathie,* p. 269.

perception represents a polarity among acts, such acts being capable of referring both to ourselves *and* to others. *This polarity is intrinsically capable of embracing the inner life of others as well as my own,* just as it embraces myself and my own experiences *in general,* and not merely the immediate present."[9]

Certain conditions, Scheler concedes, must be fulfilled before my inner perception can reveal the psychic experiences of another Ego; for instance, it is necessary that my own body undergo certain physical influences emanating from the physical body of the other. Thus, my ear must be affected by the sound waves which he sets up when he speaks to me, if I am to understand what he says. "But there is no reason why this condition *should entirely determine the act whereby these words are understood.*"[10] The conditions are understandable by the fact that to any act of possible inner perception belongs an act of possible outer perception, and that all exterior perception is grounded on an object affecting the senses. The conditions in the process of perception will therefore determine the specific content of any possible inner perception of the other's psychic experience, but in no way does this necessity of conditions fulfilled demand that perception of the other's experiences be only indirectly through analogy or empathy.

Just as our inner perception includes not only our present experience but also the whole stream of past experience as a background against which the present emerges, so does inner experience also embrace as a possibility, the whole realm of possible psychic experience as an undifferentiated stream. As the present self is perceived as emergent from the totality of past life, so does the self become aware of itself against the background of an all-embracing psychic stream which contains my experiences together with the experiences of all others. The immediacy of the social is thus posited by Scheler against the former theories of knowledge by inference. The broad scope which he allows to inner perception as the faculty of the psychic in general permits him to establish the existence of an underlying and primary total perception which gradually becomes determined by the emergence of individual psychic centers. The importance which Scheler assigns to his theory of inner perception as the heart of his theory of the perception of the other Ego, (*Wahrnehmungstheorie des fremden Ich*) is clear from the fol-

[9] *Sympathy,* p. 249. "Innere Anschauung ist also eine Akt-richtung, zu der zugehörige Akte wir uns selbst *und* Anderen gegenüber vollziehen können. Diese Akt-richtung umspannt dem 'Können' *nach von vornherein auch Ich und Erleben des Anderen,* genau so wie sie mein Ich und Erleben *überhaupt,* nicht etwa nur die unmittelbare 'Gegenwart' umspannt." *Sympathie,* p. 269.

[10] *Sympathy,* p. 249. "Diese Bedingung braucht durchaus nicht den Aktus meines Verständnisses dieser Worte eindeutig zu determinieren." *Sympathie,* p. 269.

lowing succinct statement of the inner perception of one self, "A," with respect to another, "B:"

> The act of internal perception of 'A' embraces not only his own mental processes, but has both the power and the right to take in the *whole* existing realm of minds – initially as a still unorganized stream of experiences. And just as we start by apprehending our present self against the background of our whole temporal experience, and do not manufacture it by a *synthesis* of our present self with earlier remembered states of itself, so too do we always apprehend our own self against the background of an ever-vaguer all-embracing consciousness in which our own existence and the experiences of everyone else are presented, in principle, as included together. It is not, therefore, the perception of other selves and their experiences, but only the particular content that stands out vividly at any time from this vast total content, the emergence of a self and of its experience from the great collective stream of universal consciousness, which is in fact conditioned by the bodily transactions which take place between us.[11]

That inner perception can attain the other only on condition of certain modifications having previously been undergone in the bodily sphere is in no way an argument against its immediacy, for even in the perception of my own self by inner experience certain physical conditions of the bodily sphere must be antecedent. When we turn our inner intuition on ourself then our psychic experience is revealed as detached from the total stream of the psychic only by the fact that self-experience includes a mutation or resonance in the bodily sphere. Our personal psychic experience is perceived only insofar as it is reflected further in bodily changes or at least in a *tendency to expression.* So true is this, says Scheler, that when all expression of an affective movement is suppressed, then the inner perception of it simultaneously ceases. "When joy or love are inhibited in their expression they do not simply remain the same from the internal point of view, but

[11] *Sympathy,* p. 250. "Der Akt innerer Anschauung von A umspannt nicht nur dessen eigene Seelvenvorgänge, sondern dem Rechte und der Möglichkeit nach das *gesamte* existierende Reich der Seelen – zunächst als einen noch ungegliederten Strom von Erlebnissen. Und wie wir unser Gegenwartsich von vornherein auf dem Hintergrunde des *Ganzen* unseres zeitlichen Erlebens erfassen – nicht aber erst durch *Synthesen* des Gegenwartsichs mit erinnerten früheren Ichzustanden bilden –, ebenso erfassen wir auch unser eigenes Ich immer auf dem Hintergrund eines immer undeutlicher werdenden allumfassenden Bewusstseins, in dem auch das Ichsein und Erleben aller Anderen als prinzipiell 'mitenthalten' gegeben ist. Nicht also das Wahrnehmen der fremden Iche und ihrer Erlebnisse, sondern nur der jeweilig besondere Gehalt, der uns aus diesem grossen Ganzheitsgehalt gerade lebhaft wird, das Hervortauchen eines Ich und seines Erlebens aus dem grossen Gesamtstrom des universellen Seelenlebens wäre es, was dann 'bedingt' wäre durch die Prozesse, die zwischen unseren Leibkörpern stattfinden." *Sympathie,* p. 270.

tend to evaporate."[12] If it were possible to realize the impossible, and annihilate all phenomena of expression localized in the bodily sphere, then, says Scheler, each psychic experience would still contribute to the modification of the totality of inner perception, but it would be incapable of being made the object of a particular perception.

On the basis of this equal necessity in self-perception for the fulfillment of certain physical conditions anterior to inner perception Scheler holds that the traditional priority assigned to self-perception is unfounded. All inner perception requires the fulfillment of certain physical conditions before it can become operative, and these conditions are no less imperative in self-perception than in the perception of others. "In this respect, therefore, there is, at bottom, no very crucial difference between self-awareness and the perception of mind in others. Such perception occurs, in both cases, only so far as the state of the body is modified in some way and so far as the mental state to be perceived is translated into some sort of *expression* or other physical modification."[13]

From the role which he assigns to the physical body in perception, Scheler logically rejects the two common theories of the mind-body relationship, that of cartesian dualism and the theory of psycho-physical parallelism. These theories exclude even the possibility of one self perceiving the other and the other's psychic experiences. Both theories lock man within his own psychical prison where he can apprehend only whatever the metaphysical nexus of causality might happen to project within. What such theories fail to see is that the body functions as the selector and analyst (*Analysator*) for all possible contents of inner and outer experience. The realm of the psychic as such is not causally dependent on the bodily functions; rather does it have an indirect relation to the latter as condition of the manifestation of the psychic in inner perception, a relation which exists as well for outer perception.

From the role which Scheler assigns to the body in perception he is able to make a further step in the determination of the area of possible perception of the other. Those experiences of the other Ego which we can never perceive are "other's experiences of their own *bodily states,* especially their

[12] *Sympathy,* p. 251. "Die Freude, deren Ausdruck – oder die Liebe, deren Ausdruck gehemmt wird, bleibt auch für die innere Wahrnehmung nicht etwa einfach dieselbe, sondern verflüchtigt sich." *Sympathie,* p. 271.

[13] *Sympathy,* p. 251. "Es besteht daher in diesem Punkte im Grunde gar kein so prinzipieller Unterschied zwischen der Selbst- und der Fremdwahrnehmung. Hier und dort kommt es nur zu einer solchen, sofern der Leibzustand irgendwie modifiziert wird und der wahrzunehmende Ichzustand sich in irgendeine Art des *Ausdrucks* oder irgendeiner anderen Leibmodifikation umsetzt." *Sympathie,* p. 272.

organic sensations, and the sensory feelings attached thereto."[14] It is these bodily feelings below the level of the communicable psychic, and conversely the most intimate spiritual center of man, the *Person,* which constitute the separation between one man and another. Therefore, so far as man lives directed toward his sheer bodily feelings he is incapable of sharing in the psychic life of another. On the other hand, so far as man elevates himself above the purely vegetative and lower vital sphere up towards the realm of the higher psychical and spiritual, just so far he becomes capable of sharing in a common psychic experience with another. "Hence an identical sorrow may be keenly felt . . . but never an identical sensation of pain."[15]

Scheler's theory of the original, undifferentiated psychic stream and the correlative theory of the area of inner perception constitute the basis of his explanation of the possibility of inter-ego relationships. Taken together these two theories are intended to replace the old presupposition of the priority of self-knowledge upon which the hypotheses of analogy and empathy were founded. There was, however, a second fundamental principle which these older explanations assumed as self-evident and this too, Scheler replaces by a principle of his own.

The Role of "Expression" in Perception

It was taken for granted by the defenders of analogy and empathy that my perception of the other could only reach his physical body (*Körper*) and its movements. A simple phenomenological consideration will suffice to disprove the alleged self-evident nature of this proposition, says Scheler. It is certain that we perceive the psychical level of the other through the medium of expression. We perceive directly in the smile of another his joy, in his blushing his shame, in his folded hands his prayer, in the tender glance of his eyes his love, in his words his thoughts. The objection that such knowledge is not perception can only be made when a priori theories have been set up without reference to the facts at hand; an arbitrary definition of perception as "complex of sensations" may perhaps leave no room for the phenomena of expression, but the given facts cannot be suppressed for the sake of theories.

Merleau-Ponty has recently proposed a view that is similar to Scheler's:

[14] *Sympathy,* p. 255. "... die fremden erlebten *Leibzustände,* d.h. vor allem die Organempfindungen und die mit ihnen verknüpften sinnlichen Gefühle." *Sympathie,* p. 276.

[15] *Sympathy,* p. 255. "Mann kann daher streng dasselbe Leid ... 'fühlen,' nie aber denselben Schmerz empfinden." *Sympathie,* p. 276.

"Once the prejudice of sensation has been banished, a face, a signature, a form of behavior, cease to be mere 'visual data' whose psychological meaning is to be sought in our inner experience, and the mental life of others becomes an immediate object, a whole charged with immanent meaning." [16]

Reasoned judgments Scheler points out may indeed intervene later if there arises a conflict between perceived states. It is clear, however, that such judgements are based upon data of perception. I can, for example, judge that I have misunderstood the other, or that he has attempted to deceive me by falsely expressing himself. I perceive not only the eyes of the other, but also that he watches me, or even that he watches me covertly. Thus, I can perceive that he pretends to feel what he actually does not feel, "that he is severing the familiar bond between his experience and its natural expression, and is substituting another expressive movement in place of the particular phenomenon implied by his experience." [17]

On the basis of his theory of inner perception and the fact of our perception of "expression," Scheler therefore sets forth his own solution to the question: in our perception of the other, what is it that we first perceive? What we first perceive he says, is neither the other's merely physical body (*Körper*) nor his soul, but a unified totality, as yet not distinguished in terms of inner and outer perception. Phenomena are presented to us primarily as psycho-physically indifferent; the other presents himself as accessible with equal ease to both inner and outer perception in such a way that the psychical and physical are given simultaneously. Only later, with the gradual distinction of the two areas, do we consciously advert to the presence of two types of perception. Scheler's assertion of the psycho-physical unity of the primary perception is so absolute that we shall quote here a paragraph in which he sets forth the thesis in brief.

Our immediate perceptions of our fellow-men do not relate to their bodies (unless we happen to be engaged in a medical examination), nor yet to their 'selves' or 'souls.' What we perceive are *integral wholes*, whose intuitive content is not immediately resolved in terms of internal or external perception. From this stage of givenness we can then go on, in the second place, to adopt the attitude of internal or external perception. But the fact that the individual bodily unity thus immediately presented should be associated in general with a possible object

[16] Maurice Merleau-Ponty, *Phenomenology of Perception,* trans. Colin Smith, N.Y. Humanities Press, 1962, p. 58.

[17] *Sympathy,* p. 261. . . . dass er das mir bekannte Band zwischen seinem Erleben und dessen 'natürlichen Ausdruck' zerreisst und eine andere Ausdrucksbewegung an die Stelle setzt, wo sein Erleben ein bestimmtes Ausdrucksphanomen forderte." *Sympathie,* p. 283.

accessible both to internal and external perception, is founded upon the *intrinsic* connection between these intuitive contents, a connection which also underlies my own perception of myself. It is not acquired through observation and induction from my own case.[18]

Not only the given totality appears with this characteristic of psycho-physical "indifference," but the various phenomena which arise out of it are equally of this nature. We might break these down into units of pure color-qualities, units of line, form, movement and change. We might with equal validity, however, analyze these phenomena not in terms of physical unities but in terms of the psychical. In this case, every unit of expression would be intelligible only as ordered to the total structure of the expression. But what Scheler emphasizes is that we perceive first the totality; we are given the physical and psychical simultaneously. Inner and outer perception acting on the psycho-physical unity of the living being, reveal its double nature directly. The mechanisms of the older theories of empathy and analogy, both of which were based upon the psychological assumption of associationism, were never able to yield more than a high degree of probability on the existence of other psychic centers. Their attempt to reduce the act of perception to its "component" particular sensations seemed for a time to be valid for the perception of merely physical objects. When faced with the task of reducing an "expressive whole" to the physical units which compose it, however, the theory of association revealed its deficiences. Expression is not merely the sum of its physical units; it is the revelation of a realm of psychic being transcending the purely physical and as such, its essence is to be a totality. "Hence it is intrinsically impossible ever to resolve the unity of an expressive phenomenon (such as a smile, or a menacing, kindly or affectionate look), into a sum of appearances, however large, such that its members could equally well comprise a unity of appearance in which we might

[18] *Sympathy*, p. 261–2. "Was wir an fremden Menschen, mit denen wir leben, wahrnehmen, das sind 'zunächst' weder 'fremde Körper' (sofern wir uns nicht gerade in einer äusseren ärztlichen Untersuchung befinden), noch sind es fremde 'Iche' und 'Seelen,' sondern es sind *einheitliche Ganzheiten,* die wir anschauen – ohne dass dieser Anschauungsinhalt zunächst 'zerlege' in die Richtung der 'äusseren' und 'inneren Wahrnehmung.' Wir können uns auf Grund dieser Gegebenheitsstufe dann sekundär entweder in der Richtung der äusseren oder der inneren Wahrnehmung verhalten. Dass aber mit einer solchen individuellen Leibeinheit, die uns 'zunächst' gegeben ist, überhaupt ein möglicher Gegenstand gegeben ist, der einer inneren und einer ausseren Wahrnehmung zugänglich ist, das ist im Wesenszusammenhang dieser Inhalte der Anschauung gegründet – der sogar meiner Selbstwahrnehmung bereits zugrunde liegt –, nicht aber durch Beobachtung und Induktion an mir selbst gewonnen." *Sympathie,* p. 284.

perceive merely the physical body, or a unitary impression from the physical environment."[19]

With the introduction of the factor of "expression" into the problem of intersubjectivity Scheler intends, therefore, to refute the old assumption that perception yielded nothing but the isolated physical units of the physical body (*Körper*) of the other person. This assumption was one of the difficulties upon which previous theories had always foundered. Scheler negates the entire problem by showing that *much more is immediately given in perception than had been previously allowed.* Once the factor of expression has been introduced, the necessity for calling upon projective empathy or inferential judgement is removed. The other is given immediately *qua* "living being," and we are not required to reason to this. With his analysis of the role of expression Scheler completes his phenomenological explanation of how inter-Ego relationships are possible. In a recent article, "On Perceiving Persons," by a contemporary American philosopher Frank A. Tillman, we find a theory of immediate perception very similar to Scheler's: "I propose that our perception of others is a matter of seeing a certain gesture as anger, or pain, and so on. And the problem of our knowledge of other minds is the problem of reducing the ambiguity of a particular structure with meaning."[20]

Before proceeding to a discussion of the metaphysical basis for Scheler's theory and the criticism which may be brought against this basis let us review briefly the two major points which it proposes. The first point, as we have described it above, is that of the priority of social knowledge over self-knowledge. Scheler advances this in the hypothesis of the original stream of psychic experience, at first undifferentiated into mine and thine. The second point in his theory is that of the role of expression in the perception of the other. Binding these two points together is Scheler's teaching on "inner perception." The identification of inner perception and self-perception is denied, and the field of inner perception is broadened to cover the whole area of possible psychic experience of all Egos. Outer perception, as the faculty ordered to the physical object, is complemented by inner perception, the faculty ordered to the psychical. Both types of perception coincide when

[19] *Sympathy,* p. 263–4. "Eben darum ist es wesensgesetzlich ausgeschlossen, die Einheit einer 'Ausdruckserscheinung' (z.B. ein Lächeln, ein drohendes oder gütiges oder zärtliches 'Blicken') jemals in eine noch so grosse Summe von Erscheinungen zu zerlegen, deren Glieder noch identische Einheiten waren für eine Erscheinungseinheit, in der wir den Körper bzw. eine Eindruckseinheit seitens der physischen Umwelt wahrnehmen." *Sympathie,* p. 285.

[20] Frank A. Tillman, "On Perceiving Persons," in *Phenomenology in America,* ed. James M. Edie, Chicago, Quadrangle, 1967, p. 171.

there is question of the perception of another human being; in this case outer perception grasps the physical body (*Körper*) whereas inner perception, through the expressive character of the living body (*Leib*), grasps the psychical life of the other. This latter perception is as immediate and direct as outer perception. Indeed, at the first stage, that of the "stream of experience," the psychical is known prior, and only later does one come to distinguish clearly the merely physical objects from the expressive, living beings of the world.

The Unity-of-Life Metaphysics

The hypothesis which Scheler introduces at the beginning of his theory of the perception of the other, the hypothesis of the originally undifferentiated stream of psychic experience, is perhaps the most unusual part of his teaching. We assign the reasons for this to Scheler's "unity of life" theory. We have explained earlier how, in his ethical work, Scheler had arrived at a distinction within the human being of two centers, *Person* and Ego. It is to this latter center, the Ego, that his whole theory of the "perception" of the other applies. The *Person* as we have seen, cannot become "object" of knowledge by another; we may participate in the spiritual acts of the other by "co-performing" them, but the very intimate center of the other, the *Person* cannot be totally grasped as object. Just as Scheler went to one extreme by placing the spiritual center of man beyond the reach of objective knowledge, so he went to the other extreme by reducing the vital center, the Ego, to a psychic unit immersed with others in a single stream of life.

From the time of his final rejection of Catholicism in 1922 until his death, Scheler manifests in his works an increasing tendency to bind the individual more and more tightly into some kind of supra-individual entity. We find ultimately the metaphysics of a cosmic dualism of "spirit" and "drive" (*Geist und Drang*), a position that Scheler outlined in his last work, *Man's Place in Nature*. The personal God of his Catholic era has now become mere cosmic spirit evolving under the pressure of a blind cosmic impulse or drive, with the process manifesting itself in the dualism of the vital-spiritual entity, man. At the time that he set forth the perception-theory of the other that we have described, Scheler had not yet reached this final position. We find, however, evidences of his progression in this direction, and it is due to this tendency toward a cosmic life-metaphysics that much of his thinking on the problem of the other person seems to go beyond pure phenomenological analysis. Particularly is this so in his hypothesis of the single stream of psychic life in which all Egos live.

In his analysis of the phenomenon of sympathy in *The Nature of Sympathy,* Scheler had distinguished true sympathy (*Mitgefühl*) from emotional identification (*Einsfühlung*). The discovery of these two different forms of affective intentionality, however, imposed upon Scheler the task of supplying a metaphysical explanation for them. At this period, his insistence upon the absolute individuality of the spiritual *Person,* such as we have seen it develop in his ethical research, restrained him from succumbing to any metaphysical solution which would endanger the uniqueness of the *Person.* He attempts, therefore, to account for the phenomenon of identification (*Einsfühlung*) without involving the individuality of the *Person.* Consequently the theories of absolute metaphysical monism such as those of Schelling, Hegel, or Schopenhauer, are rejected by Scheler because they fail to preserve true individuality for man's spiritual center. On the other hand, Scheler agrees that the fact of emotional identification argues to some kind of supra-individual unity. With Bergson and Driesch he settles for a unity of *life,* but he introduces an important distinction in order to save his ethical *Person.* The theory of the unity of life (*Einheit des Lebens*) is valid, he declares, only for the lower psychic center of man; it in no way touches the realm of the spiritual *Person.* On the contrary, the distinction of *Persons* is absolutely required by such phenomena as love, and any attempt to eliminate this distinction violates the evidence at hand. Love cannot be reduced either to pure sympathy (*Mitgefühl*) or identification (*Einsfühlen*). Metaphysical monism attempts such a reduction. "What has obviously happened here is that in concentrating on the phenomena of identification at the vital level, an entire *range of love-emotions* has been passed over and misunderstood. Nor, finally, is there any regard whatever here for those limits of *absolute personal privacy,* our marginal awareness of which is first quickened and made clear in the fullness and depth of love, and there alone."[21] Having safeguarded the individuality of the *Person* by denying any possibility of fusion on the level of spirit, Scheler feels free to apply a metaphysic of supra-individual unity to the vital level of man. The various types of identification and fusion which Scheler had analyzed, lead him to the conclusion that they can only be explained if some type of supra-individual unity of life is postulated. The phenomenal objects of this middle level, of this "metaphysics of organic life," can only be realized, however, by a pains-

[21] *Sympathy,* p. 71. "Man sieht sofort: Hier ist zugunsten der spezifisch vitalen Einsfühlungserscheinungen eine ganze *Wesenklasse von Liebesemotionen ignoriert* und verkannt. Endlich ist auch hier die Granze der *absolut intimen Person,* deren Grenzbewusstsein uns gerade, ja sogar ausschliesslich in der tiefsten und vollkommensten Liebe allererst aufgeht und klar wird, vollständig ignoriert." *Sympathie,* p. 78.

taking double abstraction, from man's higher spiritual acts on the one hand, and from his merely organic sensations on the other.

> Such phenomena can only appear once our powers of intellectual consciousness and corporeal sensitivity have been lulled into minimal activity. The first defines the human personality as it is in itself individual, while the second circumscribes it as 'this particular' embodied unity. It is only when man's *vital plane is isolated* to the fullest extent (never completely of course) in contrast to his purely sensory, mechanical and associative side on the one hand, and the purely cognitive level of his intellectual awareness on the other, that the above conditions are realized.[22]

Because of this necessity for preserving individuality on the level of spirit and achieving unity on the level of the vital, Scheler is obliged to reject all previous metaphysics of life which, like the *elan vital* of Bergson, demand an evolution upwards toward spirit. Equally does he reject the opposite view which would reduce the *Person* to a "mode" or "function" of a universal spirit; Fichte and Hegel have both been guilty of this latter fault, he feels.

Scheler holds rather that the individual *Person,* pure spirit, is joined in dynamic, but non-substantial fashion to a vast, single stream of life in such a way that the two different centers in man, the spiritual and the vital, can attain two totally different realms of being. The unity of the vital principle explains all the forms of affective fusion and identification between Egos which Scheler believed to be otherwise unexplainable. The undivided, incommunicable, spiritual principle explains the ethical and purely spiritual acts which Scheler had analyzed in his ethical studies. By introducing this radical dualism into the human being, he hoped to satisfy simultaneously the demands of both types of phenomena. The consequence, as Scheler admits, is to negate the substantial unity of man. "Between *spirit and life,* between person and life-centre, we discern no unity of substance, but only a bond of dynamic causality."[23] The two centers in man are thus due to two different principles. Scheler can see no other way to preserve the essence of both spirit and life. The result of a dynamic union would enable both prin-

[22] *Sympathy,* p. 73. "Erst unter Voraussetzung der möglichsten Ausschaltung der Aktualität des geistigen Wachbewusstseins *und* des Körperempfindungsbewusstseins – deren erstes die menschliche Person in sich selbst individuiert, deren zweites sie als 'diese' Leibeinheit 'singularisiert' – können ja Phanomene dieser Art auftreten, d.h. erst unter möglichster (natürlich nie voll erreichbarer) *Isolierung der Vitalschicht* des Menschen im Unterschied und Gegensatz zur rein sensuell-mechanisch-assoziativen und zur rein noetischen Schicht des geistigen Bewusstseins." *Sympathie,* p. 80.

[23] *Sympathy,* p. 76. "Kein substantiales, ein nur *dynamisch kausales Einheitsband* besteht uns zwischen Geist und Leben, Person und Lebenszentrum." *Sympathie,* p. 83.

ciples freedom of operation within their own spheres: "If . . . the connection between spirit and life is merely dynamic, it might also be the case that, although individual spirits were personal substances, life (in a sense still to be ascertained) might be metaphysically one and the same in all persons – though exerting itself dynamically in many different ways."[24]

It is to this theory of the unity of life, therefore, that we must trace Scheler's hypothesis of the common field of psychic experience. As he had himself observed, any theory of the other Ego must ultimately justify itself on a metaphysical basis. What Scheler proposes is a theory of the perception of the other on the vital level. The metaphysic which he offers in support of it, is consequently, a metaphysic operating on the level of life. In his research in the field of intersubjectivity, he had encountered certain phenomena in which human Egos seemed to merge into a psychic life. Since the spiritual *Person* was absolutely incapable of submitting to such an invasion of its individuality, he decided that another center in man, the vital-psychic, must be that part of the human being which could enter into objective psychic fusion with another. The reasons for this possibility he further decided must be the basic unity of the life-stream of all living beings.

Once given such a unity Scheler felt that he could not only explain the phenomenon of fusion, but also provide a firm basis for a theory of the perception of the other Ego, a theory which would avoid the clumsy mechanisms of the older hypotheses of empathy and inference. Since the life-stream is common and one, the psychic experiences of any individual are accessible for all who share in this common stream. Out of this vital-psychic stream the various centers emerge. Insofar as man is spirit he is individual and incommunicable, but insofar as this spirit exists under the terrestrial conditions of a spatial body, and enters into a dynamic union with the living body, man lives irrevocably in a social context with the vital-psychic centers of other men. Man is born into the stream of life, and though he gradually withdraws more and more from the complete communality of experience with the progressive development of the spirit, he always retains his position within the stream of vital-psychic life. This explains the facts of fusion and this ultimately explains for Scheler the immediacy and directness of our perception of the other Ego.

[24] *Sympathy,* p. 76. "Besteht dagegen nur die dynamische Verknüpfung von Gesit und Leben, so könnte es auch sein, dass trotz der persönlichen Substantialität der individuellen Geister das Leben in allen Personen metaphysisch ein und dasselbe Leben sei – wenn auch in seinen dynamischen Richtungen mannigfaltig gegliedert." *Sympathie,* p. 84.

Critique of Scheler's Theory

Within the limits of this very brief treatment of Scheler's theory of intersubjectivity we have unfortunately no opportunity to touch on his many brilliant insights in the whole sphere of the sociality of man and the sociology of knowledge. This would demand an extensive monograph devoted solely to that phase of Scheler's work. We have sought rather to examine the single point of Scheler's theory of intersubjectivity especially as it develops from his studies in ethics and sympathy. From such a limited study there naturally results a very limited appreciation of the range and depth of his philosophy of man. The many inconsistencies and changes of outlook which appear in Scheler's books, and which were an outward manifestation of his restless, questing spirit render particularly difficult any attempt to present an adequate and fair portrait of him at any given stage. Even before the reversal of outlook which occurred with his rejection of Catholicism, we find obscure and difficult theories put forth. Any evaluation of Scheler's theory of intersubjectivity must therefore take into consideration the fact that he never set himself the task of laboriously combing out all the inconsistencies and difficulties which beset his philosophical positions. Not the inner logic of an accepted position, but the flash of insight was his guide. With these considerations in mind, we could offer the following critical comments:

1. The primary difficulty which Scheler's theory presents is the unique splitting of the human being into the two spheres of Ego and *Person*. We are thus faced at the outset with a duality which multiples difficulties as we progress. Instead of taking man as a unit acting as a totality, Scheler separates off the spiritual sphere of pure acts, the exclusive realm of the *Person*. Below this sphere he places that of the Ego, the psychic level of life. There exists, as we have seen, only a dynamic union between these two spheres. Once having settled for this split within the human being, however, we should have expected Scheler, in treating the problem of intersubjectivity to propose a double theory to satisfy the dual nature of man. Here we are mistaken, for although Scheler proposes an elaborate theory to explain the relations possible between men on the level of Ego, there is no corresponding theory to cover the relations between *Persons*. This odd situation derives from the metaphysics of the *Person* which Scheler had established early in his ethical research and which he never later changed. The *Person* and his acts, Scheler never tires of telling us, are not "objects for knowledge" as is the psychic level of man and the "functions" pertain-

ing to that level. The spiritual center of man is transcendent to all knowledge; as that which renders objects possible, it cannot itself be made object. Whereas a man may grasp his "self" by inner perception, this does not mean that the *Person* can be object even for oneself; the *Person* of course has objective knowledge of the Ego. This seems to leave us with too thin a type of "self-knowledge," however, and Scheler almost grudgingly concedes that one "knows" his own spiritual acts by a sort of concomitant awareness which does not render them "objects."

The origin of Scheler's notion of *Person* we have traced in his ethical work. The necessity of establishing the absolutely free center of ethical acts as a correlative of the value-ethics seems to have led Scheler to extremes. Scheler's abhorrence of any "objectification" or "reification" of the spiritual *Person* results in his denial that the *Person* can ever be an object. Even Hartmann, who follows Scheler as guide in setting forth his own ethical theory, disagrees with this limitation: "If there were no possibility of a presentation of acts and persons as objects, ethics would itself be an impossibility. For man as a person is the object of ethics. And his actively transcendent acts (disposition, will, conduct) are just what is subjected to valuational judgments, they are what constitute the object of the judgment of value. Ethics takes as its object what Scheler says is incapable of becoming an object."[25]

If Scheler denies the possibility of the *Person* being an object of knowledge, he nevertheless is not prepared to admit that all knowledge of the other *Person* is thereby ruled out. Our knowledge of the other spiritual *Person* is very difficult to explain on Scheler's assumptions. We do not, according to him, make the spiritual center of the other an object of our knowledge, any more than we make his spiritual acts objects. What we do is rather co-perform his acts with him. As Schuetz expresses it: "Being merely the locus of acts the totality of which co-determines each single act, a *Person* is accessible only for another *Person* by co-achieving these acts, by thinking with, feeling with, willing with the other."[26] To explain how this is possible, however, Scheler offers no such elaborate metaphysical grounds as he had for the knowledge of the Ego-level of the other. The unproved assertion that the *Person* transcends all possible objectification is thus complemented by the equally unsubstantiated thesis of the "co-performance of acts;" the latter is an attempt to bridge the gap between *Persons* which the first assertion had set up.

It seems clear, therefore that many of Scheler's difficulties in intersub-

[25] Hartmann, *op. cit.*, Vol. I, p. 320.
[26] Schuetz, *op. cit.*, p. 325.

jective theory stem directly from his strange conception of the human being as divided into these two centers of action. By positing this separation of the spiritual and vital he seems to have involved himself in false problems which would not have appeared had he adopted a more straightforward theory of the unity of man.

2. A second major difficulty in his intersubjective theory appears in Scheler's introduction of the unity-of-life hypothesis as the metaphysical foundation for perception of the vital level of man. It is unfortunate that some of his most interesting insights are so entangled with this theory of the universal life-stream that it is difficult to extricate them. The fact of the priority of the social element in the growth of consciousness in infants does not necessarily imply the consequence that experience is presented in the beginning as a totality in which the self and others are not distinguished as different psychic centers. The possibility that one may be so directed into the life of another that reflection seldom occurs does not deny the fact that reflection is always possible and immediately reveals psychic acts as pertaining to one's self. One might question whence one derived a particular idea but this does not change the fact that at the present time the idea is now generated by and belongs to one's own self.

It is noteworthy that Scheler proposes the supra-individual consciousness as necessary only on the vital level. This widens even further the split in the human being which was set up by the *Person-Ich* duality. The vital center of man is now rooted in an amorphous life-stream and the spiritual center, independent and isolated, must operate both in its own realm and through the sphere of the vital. The theories of complete supra-personal consciousness, both biological and spiritual, which Scheler had rejected, as least were not faced with the problem which he has made for himself, of joining together a universal vital consciousness and a strictly individual spiritual consciousness in each human individual. Beyond stating that there exists a "dynamic union" between them, Scheler does not explain how any real unity could possibly arise out of a juncture of two such heterogeneous spheres of being.

The tendency of Scheler to fit man into larger and larger units of supra-individual social being is up to a certain point justifiable. Man does exist within society and is bound organically to certain definite types of society. The ever-present danger in Scheler, however, is that too great an emphasis is placed upon the constitution of man by social context to the detriment of the metaphysically inviolable boundaries of the individual. Eventually, Scheler designates even social groups as *Persons,* something which could only be admitted if the word *Person* is used in a broadly analogous sense;

certainly Scheler's concept of the free ethical *Person* cannot be transferred unchanged to designate social groups.

These criticisms are not intended to deny that Scheler has made positive contributions to the study of intersubjectivity. His analysis of the role of expression, for example, seems to be a legitimate phenomenological advance. And one cannot read Scheler's studies of man's social dimensions without agreeing that our knowledge of the other individual is more immediate and direct than one might at first suspect. After Scheler has explored the inherent difficulties of any theory of mediate, inferential knowledge, and after he has exposed the depth of the given data, it seems necessary to admit that our knowledge of others must be achieved in some special way, a way that differs vastly from our knowledge about the purely physical sphere of being.

Scheler's investigations might be taken as providing clues that could be followed up by other phenomenologists. Thus, without in any way endorsing the unity-of-life metaphysics, one could explore further the implications of such phenomena as expression, or emotional identification, and the negative emotional phenomena such as aversion and hostility. Especially today, with our new awareness of the fact of individual and group emotional stress, one might find useful the initial analyses of such phenomena as presented by Scheler.

In the case of Sartre and of Scheler, the suspicion may arise that some of their phenomenological analyses seem aimed at ratifying a previously accepted theory of being rather than at simply providing us with a pure dissection of the essential structures of experience. Thus, Sartre's ontology of nothingness restricts him to an analysis of frustration situations in which subjects are foredoomed to failure in their attempts to reach another subject. And Scheler's unity-of-life theory enables him to see all subjects ontologically linked to one another through participation in a single cosmic stream of psychic life. One wonders if the opposite, but equally extreme positions of Sartre and Scheler on intersubjectivity are not greatly influenced by the specific ontologies that encumber their phenomenologies.

In the following section we shall examine a phenomenology of intersubjectivity provided by another of Husserl's early disciples, Dietrich von Hildebrand. Although von Hildebrand is basically oriented toward an Augustinian religious outlook, his analysis of intersubjectivity seems to depend less on any antecedent metaphysics, to stay closer to simple experience, and to manifest less of the system-building tendency that one finds in Sartre and Scheler. As a consequence, its conclusions are less sweeping, but may for that reason appear to be closer to the early ideal of eidetic phenomenology as a patient probing of the structures of man's lived world of experience.

SECTION THREE

DIETRICH VON HILDEBRAND
THE PHENOMENOLOGY OF LOVE

CHAPTER VI

ENCOUNTER AND UNION BETWEEN PERSONS

Dietrich von Hildebrand had studied with Husserl at Göttingen in the 1909–1914 period and was teaching at Munich until banned by the Nazis, when like many other German intellectuals he emigrated to the United States.

Most of Husserl's students of that era – von Hildebrand included – had been attracted by the eidetic phenomenology that Husserl had developed in his early period. Many of them saw it as opening the way to a viable realism and thus providing another option to both an empty Kantian formalism and a reductivistic psychologism. Understandably then, they were increasingly disturbed by Husserl's turn toward idealism and his almost exclusive concentration on the theory of the transcendental Ego. "To the first announcement of Husserl's phenomenological transcendentalism and idealism the group responded with growing consternation."[1]

In the following three decades, therefore, Husserl and his early students developed phenomenology in different fashion. He moved ever deeper into the analysis of transcendental consciousness. But most of his Göttingen students continued to practice phenomenology as a method for the identification and description of the essential structures of objective experience. Among these Göttingen eidetic phenomenologists von Hildebrand was most emphatic in holding a realistic viewpoint.

He sees phenomenology as opposed to any idealism and declares that his own phenomenological analysis "signifies in fact the most outspoken objectivism and realism."[2] Phenomenology in his realistic sense "is neither a

[1] Herbert Spiegelberg, *The Phenomenological Movement, A Historical Introduction,* 2 vols., The Hague, Nijhoff, 1965, Vol. I, p. 170.

[2] Dietrich von Hildebrand, *What is Philosophy*?, Milwaukee, Bruce, 1960, p. 223. This book gives a succinct statement of von Hildebrand's views on the nature of philosophical knowing as an apriori grasp of intelligible essences. The book is basically a slightly revised formulation of his epistemological position as set forth in an earlier work, *Der Sinn Philosophischen Fragens und Erkennens,* Bonn, Hanstein, 1950. This

reduction of the world to mere phenomena, nor a mere description of appearances."[3] Furthermore, as opposed to many other modern philosophical methods, phenomenology places its emphasis "on the existential, immediate intuitive contact with the object, in opposition to any mere abstractionism or any dealing with mere concepts."[4]

He has thus been constant in emphasizing that phenomena often dismissed as "merely subjective" are as objective as any physical fact. "To be subjective may mean, first of all, to pertain to the personal world, as opposed to the impersonal world . . . An act of knowledge, an act of will, an act of love or joy are subjective in this sense . . . But let it be clearly marked and known: the act of knowing, loving and so forth, are fully objective *realities*. They are at least as 'real' as a stone or a tree. Thus the term 'subjective' refers to the ontological feature of being a 'subject' and a person, and not to the epistemological feature of being an appearance *for* a subject."[5]

In fact, in assessing the ontological value attaching to this subjective order of being, von Hildebrand would rank it far above that of impersonal being. "We may go still further and say that these subjective beings, these personal entities, are superior in being to the objective, nonpersonal beings. They possess a higher being and are even more 'real.'"[6] Therefore he holds that, depending on the context, one may legitimately speak of the acts of the subject as either subjective or objective. When we say that they are subjective, we mean that they occur in the subjective, personal realm of being.

latter work was itself in process of publication and in galley proofs until halted by the Nazi regime with its proscription of publications by political opponents. Since von Hildebrand fled to Vienna and later the United States, the early German version (written in 1932) was not actually published until after the war. Representing as it does, however, von Hildebrand's views in 1932, it gives evidence of the vigorous opposition to Husserl's idealistic phenomenology that was so widespread among his students of the early Göttingen years. The following paragraph expresses this opposition viewpoint in brief:

"Der Ausdruck Phänomenologie ist heute schon vieldeutig geworden. Husserl hat in seinen *Ideen zu einer reinen Phänomenologie und phänomenologischen Philosophie* (1913; Nachwort dazu 1930) und entschiedener noch in seiner *Formalen und transzendentalen Logik, Versuch einer Kritik der logischen Vernunft* (1929) eine immer stärkere Wendung zum Idealismus kantischer Prägung hin vollzogen, durch die er den Boden der Phänomenologie, wie sie in der ersten Auflage der *Logischen Untersuchungen* vertreten wurde, verlassen hat. Wenn wir hier von 'Phänomenologie' reden, so geschieht dies nur im Sinne der intuitiven Wesensanalyse, wie sie vor allem in den Arbeiten von Adolf Reinach, Alexander Pfänder, Hedwig Conrad Martius und des Verfassers zu finden ist." p. 90.

[3] von Hildebrand, *What is Philosophy*?, p. 223.

[4] *Ibid.*, p. 224.

[5] *Ibid.*, p. 153–4.

[6] *Ibid.*, p. 154.

And, "when subjective is used in this ontological sense of personal, it clearly escapes all the suspicions attaching to the epistemological use of the term." [7]

These same human acts of a subject may, in an epistemological sense, be said to be objective; i.e. they are real occurences taking place in a sphere of real, though personal, being. Furthermore, the objectivity of these acts can be seen from the fact that some of them, e.g., promises or contracts, create a bond between persons, a bond that is as objective and real as any physical bond. And in fact, if the sphere of personal being ranks higher ontologically than nonpersonal reality, then we may say that human acts and the bonds that they create are more real and objective than any nonpersonal occurences.

But does it not seem rather odd to call intersubjective relationships real and objective? It does, von Hildebrand admits, but this is because there is a kind of subtle and unrecognized materialism guiding our thinking. We tend to identify the real and objective with what can be encompassed within the boundaries of a material thing. One might illustrate his point with a physical analogy: No one would deny the reality and objectivity either of a magnet's radiating field of force, or of the consequent physical bonds of attraction it forms with certain other metal bodies. Yet the field of force and the bonds of attraction are not contained within the actual boundaries of the visible physical magnet. So von Hildebrand would see no reason to deny that certain acts of the human subject create, analogously, a unique radiating social field of force which is just as real and objective, and which creates social bonds or interpersonal relationships that are just as real and objective, as physical ones.

Thus, as with many of those who took their direction from the early work of Husserl, von Hildebrand sees phenomenology as "the intuitive analysis of genuine, highly intelligible essences." [8] These constitute the invariant structures of our lived experience; they are consequently a priori; and they can be detected and identified only by careful reflection on the varying content of concrete human acts.

We cannot give here a complete presentation of von Hildebrand's phenomenological theory. We may note, however, that he does not view phenomenology as a newly created mode of philosophizing; he regards it as simply a modern version of what is at the heart of all the great philosophies of the past. "It is rather the approach which is at the basis of every great

[7] *Ibid.*, p. 154.
[8] *Ibid.*, p. 223.

philosophical discovery."[9] But though the great philosophers have always used the phenomenological method, they have done so in a non-systematic fashion. Contemporary phenomenology for von Hildebrand therefore, is marked by a conscious attempt to make a consistent method out of an ancient practice.

Like Scheler, by whom he was influenced, von Hildebrand is less concerned with the study of neutral, nonpersonal reality than he is with the ethical and social world. But his analysis of man's social and affective dimension does not appeal, as does Scheler's, to an extra-phenomenological unity-of-life metaphysics. Nor do we find the elaborate construction of the *Person-Ich* distinction that is necessitated by Scheler's life-philosophy and that accounts for his curious double theory of intersubjectivity in which men are seen to be united in a kind of pan-vitalism and yet radically individual and separate at the level of spirit.

Von Hildebrand does subscribe, however, to a theory of value-ethics that is similar to Scheler's. Thus, value-perception is given equal rank with other modes of cognition; values themselves function as the condition for the development of positive interpersonal relationships, and values are conceived to have objective ontological status. "According to Scheler, Hartmann, Von Hildebrand, and others, such values are to be *discovered in* things and not to be *imposed on* things by an observing – and evaluating – subject. And the techniques for discovering them are to be the phenomenological techniques of objective analysis and description, resulting in an '*intuition*' of value essences (essential values)."[10]

Von Hildebrand's analysis of intersubjectivity therefore, will be a systematic attempt (a) to uncover and describe the specific invariant structure (or essence) of those various bonds of community that exist among persons; and (b) an attempt also to identify the essence of the human acts from which communal relationships arise. Both these acts and the communal bonds generated by them are considered as objective and real in the sense discussed above. Von Hildebrand has given a systematic presentation of his views on intersubjectivity in his *Die Metaphysik der Gemeinschaft*,[11] and this will be the main source of our study.

It has often been noted that the phenomenological analyses of Husserl's transcendental period are unbelievably obscure and difficult. But this is usually not true of his early writings and of the work of his early disciples.

[9] *Ibid.*, p. 223.
[10] Quentin Lauer, *op. cit.*, p. 10.
[11] von Hildebrand, *Die Metaphysik der Gemeinschaft*, Regensberg, Habbel, 1954. This will be cited as *MG*.

Thus, one finds that the phenomenological analyses of Scheler and von Hildebrand often start with a simplicity and ease that is deceptive. Von Hildebrand especially begins with ordinary, easily recognizable experiences, and by a patient dwelling on an act or a situation strives to "do justice" to this thematic object by letting the latent meaning and unity of its structure emerge. For, as he explains, "Besides its existential contact with reality, phenomenology is further characterized by its facing the object itself and by its methodical concern to do justice to the *qualitative* nature of the object."[12]

Bringing out the qualitative nature of the object involves the dissection of the essential traits of experience through a process of description and distinctions. But the description of the phenomenologist is not a haphazard one. What the American philosopher James Edie has said recently of the function of phenomenological description expresses succinctly the view held by von Hildebrand and the early eidetic phenomenologists. Discussing a series of essays on the eidetic analysis of social relationships, Edie remarks: "What these and similar phenomenological studies have in common, and must have in common under pain of lapsing into mere, undirected empirical description and fact-finding, is the phenomenological aim to elucidate eidetic structures, certain structural conditions of human (social) experience. Concrete and well-chosen paradigm cases and examples are found, as in a Platonic dialogue, which will illustrate the range of eidetic possibilities of a given modality of experience. But such concrete examples and descriptions are only the means of access to the underlying *a prioris* of experience which ultimately account for them. It is these *a prioris* or eidetic structures of experience which a phenomenological investigation attempts to thematize."[13]

In addition to providing essential descriptions, von Hildebrand's analyses are rich with distinctions of differences between the disclosed structures of experience. This tendency toward manifold distinctions has warrant, too, in the original eidetic method of Husserl. For, as Farber has remarked, if we were to judge the meaning of phenomenology from Husserl's early work, the *Logical Investigations,* "one important aspect of phenomenology might well be defined as the art of making, or finding distinctions . . . Where we are accustomed to finding simplicity, a very complex situation is shown to exist; and after numerous distinctions have been drawn carefully, the reader is made to feel that only a beginning has been made."[14]

[12] von Hildebrand, *What is Philosophy*?, p. 225.
[13] James Edie, *op. cit.,* p. 25.
[14] Farber, *op. cit.,* p. 216.

Even making a beginning, however, requires effort – a point which should perhaps be noted. For, because of their use of such terms as "intuit" and "see," phenomenologists from the beginning have often been taken, mistakenly, to mean that the essential traits of experience would flash into view with a moment's intellectual attention. But phenomenology does not propose instant insight. Findlay has remarked aptly that "the experience of eidei (essences) and their necessary relations must be dialectical; it must arise in the active rubbing together of words, illustrations, and rough ideas, and not through any merely passive glance." [15] This, then, is the method that we find von Hildebrand using in the analysis of intersubjectivity that we are about to examine. He progresses slowly, attempting to describe and distinguish different levels and dimensions of interpersonal relationships in order to arrive at the essence of each type.

Phenomenological analysis, as we have stressed, is of various kinds. Husserl's analyses of transcendental subjectivity, for example, are almost as abstract and dry as his dissection of logical categories. But not all phenomenologists have Husserl's mathematical background and bent. Von Hildebrand and others who see phenomenology as concerned not with transcendental subjectivity but with man's lived world of experience tend to be more concrete and descriptive. With phenomenological analyses of this latter kind there arises a special problem when one attempts an accurate exposition of the content of such descriptive analyses.

There is the risk that a mere abstract condensation will fail to deliver to the reader the precise essence that the analyst is trying to capture, for the meaning and the structure of the experience cannot be exhibited like an abstract mathematical formula. It can only be grasped as the pattern that emerges *through and with* the detail of the description. The eidetic phenomenologist does not pluck out an essence and hold it up for viewing totally isolated from its context. For the essence does not exist "in the abstract," but only as the structural element in the living tissue of human acts and attitudes. And so one cannot pull apart the gossamer web of living experience looking for an eidos.

Ideally, therefore, one should read such phenomenological descriptions in full, even if only in translation for those that were originally composed in another language. This is possible with some of the major works of both Sartre and Scheler. Unfortunately, however, von Hildebrand's most extensive treatment of intersubjectivity has not yet been translated from the German. Our exposition of the various intersubjective situations that he anal-

[15] J. N. Findlay, "Essential Probabilities" in *Phenomenology in America*, p. 99.

yzes may create the impression, therefore, that he provides merely a set of dry categories removed from living experience. But the reader should bear in mind that the nature of expository writing makes it almost impossible to convey the flavor and nuances of the detailed descriptions found in the original.

The Paradox of Subjectivity

In his lengthy phenomenological study of man as a being of community, von Hildebrand does not confine himself merely to an analysis of one-to-one interpersonal relationships. He goes beyond these to analyze the larger communities into which one is integrated as a member of a family and of civil society. In all cases he attempts to identify essential formal differences in the search for the eidos of each kind of intersubjective situation. Our study of his views, however, will be limited to an examination of what he has to say about those most basic intersubjective relationships that make all larger forms of community possible.

Von Hildebrand begins his analysis by calling attention to "the paradox of subjectivity." If we compare the human being with other beings in our experienced world, he points out, we come upon a noteworthy fact: Man displays a unique ontological ambivalence with respect to intersubjectivity. For he appears simultaneously as the most completely self-contained being that we can identify, and yet as the one most open to the deepest union with other beings. He exists both for himself and for community with others. He is thus paradoxically complete and yet incomplete in a way not paralleled by any non-human being. Since von Hildebrand feels that any phenomenology of subjectivity must take account of this paradox without attempting to eliminate it through some form of reductionism, he dwells at some length on each dimension of man's ambivalence, discussing first man's unique self-identity.

The unusual nature of human individuality, he feels, can best be appreciated if we compare the human being's self-identity with that which we find among beings in the purely material sphere and in the sphere of living, but non-human beings. For there are gradations in the degree of "wholeness" and individuality that each kind of being manifests.

At the lowest level of purely material being we find a thin kind of self-identity and wholeness. Any material thing possesses an inner homogeneity that to some extent distinguishes it from the matter of its environment. But its self-identity is a precarious one – its components can at any moment disintegrate and merge with the physical continuum of nature. Thus, though the purely physical being has self-identity it cannot unite with another being under threat of losing its individuality.

When we consider an organism, the situation is somewhat different. Though its contingency in existence is in some ways even greater than a non-living thing – for its dependencies are more extensive – nevertheless it has a much more distinct individuality. For one thing, the limits that mark it off from its environment are more clearly visible. Furthermore, it has its own internal fullness of being. For it continues to exist by a self-contained cycle of successive internal changes. This gives it more of an inner wholeness, a more genuine individuality than any non-living thing. For all the elements making it up are bound together with such cohesion and internal relationship that the boundaries of its specific being are more definite. Whereas with merely physical things, we can distinguish them as emerging from the background of a generic, universal "stuff," the organism does not appear to be a simple instance of a universal "life-stuff."

Von Hildebrand is thus emphatic in denying the unity-of-life thesis of Scheler. There is no phenomenological justification he feels, for postulating some "stream of common life" in which all living things participate, analogous to the basic material substratum out of which physical things emerge and to which they return. For a comparison of the different degrees of self-identity and wholeness exhibited by things and organisms clearly brings out the much greater ontological unity and independence of the living thing. The material substance is merely a contingent part separated out from the general mass of matter; the organism on the contrary, is a genuine individual, governed by an inner, unifying principle.

Continuing his comparison of the varying types of self-sufficiency found among beings he considers, finally, the human being. Here the notion of self-possession and of being-in-itself reaches a completely new level. For with man we reach a person – a free, conscious being, gifted with an Ego, who has a full measure of self-possession extending even to the power of self-reflection. He is complete "world-in-himself" exhibiting a wholeness that is found at no other level of being. Von Hildebrand emphasizes that we find in man a far greater degree of independence in being over against the environing situation. "The complete and balanced unity, the homogeneity of every constitutive factor, the sharp delimitation and demarcation from every other individual are the particularly obvious characteristics of man." [16] All

[16] "Die völlig in sich abgeschlossene Einheit, die von jedem Element des Zufälligen freie innere Zusammengehaltenheit, die scharfe Abgegrenztheit und Abgesetztheit gegenüber jedem anderen Individuum sind ohne weiteres als Charaktere dieser Substanz ersichtlich." *MG,* p. 20.

of these factors go to make up the basis for his dignity as a personal being, expressing in the highest way the ideal of a self-sufficient individual being.

Here, too, he points out one must guard against any form of reductionism – even though in this case a "spiritual" reductionism – that would ignore the inerradicable uniqueness of each person and attempt to demonstrate that the person is constituted out of some kind of spiritual continuum, as in classical pantheism. This is analogous on the level of spirit to the pan-vitalism we have seen advanced by Scheler. Such pan-spiritualism, von Hildebrand sees rooted in the attempted extrapolation of material models into the world of spirit.

This, therefore, is what he means by designating man as a "world-in-himself": The person exhibits the highest degree of self-identity of any being. His individuality is such that any erasure of the boundaries that mark off one person from another is impossible. "Persons cannot like elements of a continuum, melt into a unity, nor can they be genuine 'parts' of a whole."[17] That unity, achieved by disintegration of individuality, which purely physical beings can attain, is impossible for persons.

This inviolable individuality of the person is the first element in the "paradox of subjectivity" that von Hildebrand points out. The second – seemingly at odds with the first – is the fact that despite this unique self-containedness the person appears to find fulfillment of his being only through "spiritual contact" with other persons and through union with them. Any adequate phenomenological consideration of the total being of the person reveals these two polarities: he is the uniquely self-contained being and at the same time the one who must have community with others. "We find that although man is still a 'world-for-himself' he must transcend himself by contact with other persons; there is effected thereby a much deeper union with them than if each were to become lost in the other, and a much deeper union than the parts of any continuum achieve."[18]

When we consider phenomenologically such apparently ordinary situations as mutual conversation, a question-and-answer dialogue, or the exchange of words of mutual love, something more than the ordinary comes to light. For we realize that when one person directs himself in such a meaningful way to another and simultaneously grasps the other's similar direction toward him, there has been created a new kind of "contact" be-

[17] "Personen können nie wie Elemente eines Kontinuums zu einer Einheit verschmelzen . . .," MG, p. 20.

[18] "Und so finden wir denn auch, dass der Mensch, obgleich eine so ausgeprägte Welt für sich, die Möglichkeit besitzt, transzendierend andere Personen in einer Weise zu berühren, die eine viel tiefere Verbindung mit ihnen darstellt als jenes äussere Aneinanderschliessen, das die Teile eines Kontinuums verbindet." *MG.*, p. 21.

tween these two beings. And through this contact a new mode of unity can arise that is far different and far deeper than any unity effected by the merely external conjunction of parts in a whole. For what we have in the case of persons is not a mere "contact" or "touching," but a genuine "encounter," a form of meeting that is possible only for persons.

One might note here that Heidegger has given a somewhat similar phenomenological description of the difference between the way in which two physical things touch one another and the unique kind of encounter that only the human being (*Dasein*) can achieve.[19] But although Heidegger affirms that man's being is always a "being-with" (*Mitsein*), he does not provide the kind of detailed analysis of the forms of "being-with" such as we find in von Hildebrand.[20]

The brief consideration we have made of the "paradox of subjectivity" has not dissolved the paradox – it has only deepened it. For it is clear that although many lesser modes of union, proper to lower realms of being, are impossible for personal beings, nevertheless, by effecting a contact with other personal beings the person can create a type of unity that far surpasses all those possible among nonpersonal beings. This special mode of human contact – the encounter – von Hildebrand submits to phenomenological analysis.

Essential Types of Encounter

The modes of encounter that von Hildebrand's analysis reveals are numerous, both in their variety and their depth. Prior to an actual encounter, however, there is first what he calls the "non-revealed attitude." In this we assume a specific emotional attitude toward another person, we direct ourselves inwardly to the other, without however manifesting this attitude to him. This is a common experience that everyone can testify to. For example, we are angry with someone, or we have a feeling of affection for someone, but we do not allow this to be expressed. Von Hildebrand sees this as a genuine mode of personal being, not a mere psychological state without ontological relevance. For we are not simply performing a psychic act, but we are directing our whole being toward the other in a specific fashion. We are now "being-toward" him. In phenomenological language, we assume an "intentional" relationship to him.

This non-revealed intentional attitude toward the other does not yet constitute an encounter. For we do not yet as von Hildebrand says, penetrate

[19] Heidegger, *Sein und Zeit,* p. 55, *Being and Time,* p. 81.

[20] See *Sein und Zeit,* p. 113, sq., *Being and Time,* p. 149, sq., for Heidegger's analysis of Being-with.

the "interpersonal space" that exists between persons. Therefore he describes this as not constituting a "real" relationship between persons, but merely an "intentional" one. As mentioned earlier, von Hildebrand insists that there are interpersonal relationships that ontologically deserve the designation of "real and objective," with at least as much right as do physical relationships. But the non-revealed attitude does not yet suffice to establish a *real* intersubjective situation. For it is still only an intending by one subject that has not yet reached out to encounter the other. When this intentional attitude *is* expressed and reaches the other we then establish an objective and real intersubjective situation. And, depending on the specific situation, various degrees of reality will be distinguished as we shall see.

Once again, says von Hildebrand, a comparison with the way in which we can touch a purely physical thing is illustrative. For when we literally touch such an object, there is no possibility for an encounter, since there is no potential reciprocity. When the other being that we contact by a revealed attitude is a person, however, the situation is totally different. For there is now the possibility for this person to assimilate consciously my revealed attitude and thus establish between us a new state-of-affairs. His reception of my intending and his reaction to it brings a real, objective intersubjective situation to birth. Furthermore, the nature of physical beings allows for only one mode of contact between them – they can be physically juxtaposed. But the nature of persons, who possess the power of intending in manifold ways, makes possible the establishment of different kinds of intersubjective situations with different degrees of reality. This opens up a whole realm of social reality to phenomenological investigation. Von Hildebrand proposes, therefore, to explore the various essential types of intersubjective situations that can be identified.

The first and most basic distinction he discusses is that between a revealed attitude and a "social act." The analysis of the social act was first made by Adolph Reinach, a contemporary of von Hildebrand's at Göttingen, and was later discussed by a number of early phenomenologists.[21] As Reinach pointed out, when one subject communicates with another, as for example by questioning, by promising, or requesting, these acts exhibit the a priori structure of "intending the other." The essence of the act includes the expectation of its being received by the addressee. Unless this intention of reaching the other is meant, we do not have a social act.

[21] For a brief discussion of Reinach's analysis of the social act, see Spiegelberg, *op. cit.*, I, p. 203. The original statement is Adolph Reinach, "Die apriorischen Grundlage des bürgerlichen Rechtes," in *Jahrbuch für Philosophie und phänomenologische Forschung*, Vol. I, Halle, 1913.

The social act, therefore, creates an intersubjective situation. For the interpersonal space between the two persons is penetrated and a new bipolar relationship established in which both beings function as subjects. Here then we have for von Hildebrand the first level of encounter between subjects. But in the social act only a minimal kind of encounter is present. "For in a social act, the other person is only the one who is 'addressed,'" and the link between us is due to the fact that "we have a common object that stands between us."[22] In the social act I communicate an objective content, and therefore it is not the other person *qua* person but the communicated content that dominates the situation. And this intention of communicating an objective content puts the social act in a different category from the expressed attitude. For in the latter there is found, not the intention of communicating a neutral content, but the intending of one's being as such toward the other, as being-angry, or being-affectionate.

For Von Hildebrand, therefore, the revealed attitude establishes a completely new and distinct type of interpersonal situation. For the "content" of the expressed attitude is not neutral information, but our being-for-the-other as it is at that moment. We exhibit now what was not visible before, our being-toward him. "We may think, for instance, of the case in which someone meets a bitter enemy and now at last finds the opportunity to reveal his hatred to him, either by word or look or deed; his hatred flashes out like flame and sears the other."[23]

Von Hildebrand is concerned to establish the revealed attitude as an essential type of act, a genuine eidetic structure irreducible to others. He tests its unity-structure, therefore by probing possible ways in which it could be regarded as a mere compound of other acts. Could it, for example, be regarded as a combination of a previously unrevealed attitude plus a social act? This does not seem to be the case. For in social acts there is always the communication of an objective content. Clearly, of course, this content could be a fact about myself – that I feel happy or sad, or even that I love or hate the other. But merely communicating facts about myself does not suffice to constitute a revealed attitude. "The specific characteristic of the revealed attitude is that the communication and the message manifest an

[22] "Aber andererseits ist die fremde Person im sozialen Akt nur 'Adressat,' . . . wir haben einen gemeinsamen Gegenstand, der gleichsam zwischen uns steht." *MG.*, p. 25.

[23] "Denken wir an den Fall, dass jemand seinem Feinde begegnet und endlich Gelegenheit findet, ihm seinen Hass zu verlautbaren, sei es durch Worte, Blicke, Gebärden oder Taten, den andern mit dem ätzenden Strahl seines Hasses ausdrücklich zu treffen." *MG.*, p. 26.

organic whole. It is not concerned with the fact *that* I love or hate, but the attitude itself breaks forth and actually reaches the other person."[24]

The irreducible unity of act and content in the revealed attitude, von Hildebrand points out, testifies to the fact that in it I am expressing a mode of my being – and my very being reaches out to the other. "I find myself in the very execution of my attitude; I find myself *in* my hatred or *in* my love."[25]

There is a further difference between a mere communicative social act and a genuine revealed attitude. The latter can only be achieved in the presence of the one whom it concerns. For the very meaning of the revealed attitude is to allow my being-toward-him to reach him directly.

Continuing his analysis of the essence of the revealed attitude, von Hildebrand next distinguishes it from two allied phenomena. There is first that almost automatic external expression of emotion that accompanies emotional states. Normally we express our basic emotional state in certain physical ways without being aware of the fact. Indeed, it is often true that only if for some reason we wish not to let this automatic expression appear do we become aware of it, because we are conscious of the effort to suppress it. The differences between such automatic expression and the genuine revealed attitude are two: The revealed attitude is always something of which we are fully aware. And furthermore, it is always directed to another person as such, whereas the automatic expression of emotion functions whether the emotive act is directed at another or not.

Another mode of act to be distinguished from the genuine revealed attitude is that in which a person consciously and willfully indulges in undirected emotional expression for its own sake. This exhibits more the character of a dynamic drive rather than an intentional act aimed at another. For the object of it is not to reach another person, but simply to indulge oneself in an emotive way. It appears as the accompaniment of strong emotional experiences rather than as their dominant theme.

To summarize, therefore, von Hildebrand sees the revealed attitude as a specific structure of the interpersonal situation whose essence can be clearly distinguished from other allied phenomena. It exhibits a unity that cannot be compounded from social acts of communication. Nor is it reducible to the class of automatic emotive expressions, whether conscious or unconscious. It possesses its own unique structure:

[24] "Gerade das ist aber das Charakteristikum der verlautbarten Stellungnahme, dass Stellungnahme und Kundgabe ein organisches Ganzes darstellen. Nicht um den Sachverhalt, *dass* ich hasse oder liebe, handelt es sich; sondern die Stellungnahme selbst wird 'laut,' erreicht die andere Person 'wirklich." *MG.*, p. 27.

[25] ". . . ich befinde mich dabei im Voll*zug* der Stellungnahme, ich 'befinde' mich *in* meinem Hass oder *in* meiner Liebe." *MG.*, p. 27.

Rather, it represents a new level of contact beyond the unrevealed attitude; it consists in speaking forth the 'inner word' to the person addressed, that 'word' which is immanently enclosed in every attitude toward the other person; it is a true case of the attitude itself coming into full conscious act. Even more, it pertains to the full essence of this encounter that the other person not only take notice of my attitude, but that he be truly touched by its content.[26]

Given the existence of a revealed attitude, von Hildebrand sees four possible situations that can develop. These indicate different degrees of depth and reality that may characterize the interpersonal relationships set up by the revealed attitude. Using as our example a revealed attitude of love, we may describe them briefly as follows:

In the first instance, the person from whom the revealed attitude of love originates may find that the other person receives this revelation but does not treat it according to its specific essence *as* a revelation of the being of the person making it. Rather he treats it more like a communication. He accepts it almost as he might receive information about a situation in which he was not involved. He does not grasp the revealed attitude of love as intended to meet him on the level of his very being.

In the second instance, the revealed love is not received as a communication of information. It is grasped for what it truly is. But the recipient does not reciprocate with a loving response. Rather he ignores the expression of love or perhaps even responds with an opposite attitude of his own. He is irritated by the proffer of love and refuses it.

We may have a third situation in which the revealed attitude is not only recognized for what it is, but is positively received by the other person. The full intention directing the revelation is encompassed.

The last situation is one in which the revealed love is not only received in the full sense but there is also a return of love manifested from the other person. The essential structure of this situation is the mutuality of revelation. We have here the highest instance of personal encounter.

All four of these situations are of the general "I-Thou" type. But there are definitely different depths to this kind of relationship depending on which of the situations is realized. Furthermore, it should be noted that though we use love as our example, the same *formal* structure would be

[26] "Vielmehr ist sie etwas prinzipiell Neues gegenüber der stillen Stellungnahme, – nämlich das Laut-werden des 'inneren Wortes' dem Adressaten gegenüber, jenes 'Wortes,' das in jeder fremdpersonalen Stellungnahme immanent enthalten ist, ein wirkliches Heraustreten 'meiner' Stellungnahme bis zu dem 'andern' hin. Und darüber hinaus gehört notwendig zu ihrer *vollen* Konstitution, dass der andere von meiner Intention nicht nur schlicht 'Kenntnis nimmt,' sondern von dem eigentümlichen 'Stoff' meiner Stellungnahme wirklich *betroffen* wird." *MG.*, p. 30.

found if hatred constituted the matter of the revelation. We would still have an I-Thou relationship progressing through four stages, but it would be the reverse of love. To render even more concrete the differences between the formally distinct situations that a revealed attitude may give rise to, von Hildebrand suggests an analogy with the situations that may arise from our looking at another person.

The analogy can serve us here not only to illustrate von Hildebrand's analysis of the eidetic difference between the types of I-Thou situations, but it also provides an interesting comparison with Sartre's treatment of "the look," that we have discussed earlier. For where Sartre interprets the looking-situation as always one of hostility and attempted dominance, von Hildebrand's more formal phenomenological analysis allows him to credit the revealed attitude and thus the look, with a material content of either love or hatred. It should be kept in mind, however, that for von Hildebrand the look does not have the same ontological significance that Sartre attaches to it. Rather it is simply one small element of expressiveness in general in which we can see the whole revealed attitude of the person symbolized in a minor way. He draws the analogy in this fashion:

> We look at someone, but he does not notice it. Here we have [what would correspond to] the first degree [of a revealed attitude] – the purely intentional and not the real contact. If he notices my look, but does not return it, the second degree. If he looks at my face at the same time that I look at his, the third degree. If, however, our looks meet and simultaneously interpentrate to reach the person of the other, then there is effected a quite specific [analogy to the] encounter of spirits, the formal climax of expressed mutual relatedness.[27]

Up to this point we have been discussing what von Hildebrand calls the most primary interpersonal situation, "encounter" between two individuals. And, though he illustrates his distinctions between different essential types of encounter by the example of a love or hate encounter, the analysis itself is intended purely as a formal one. He has been primarily concerned to show that human beings can contact one another in a way that no nonpersonal beings can – by an intentional attitude that can be expressed and reach the other. The mode of contact between nonpersonal beings is single;

[27] "Wir blicken jemand an, und er merkt es nicht. Hier haben wir die unterste Stufe – gleichsam die nur intentionäre und nicht reale Berührung. Wenn er es merkt ohne mich anzublicken, die zweite. Wenn er mein Gesicht zu derselben Zeit ansieht wie ich das seine, die dritte. Wenn sich unsere Blicke aber begegnen und – gleichsam ineinander geschoben – die Person des andern erreichen, so liegt eine ganz einzigartige geistige Berührung vor, ein formaler Höhepunkt des ausdrücklichen Aufeinanderbezogenseins." *MG.*, p. 32.

that between intentional beings admits of a range of encounters that are structually different.

Basic Types of Union

In addition to this first intersubjective situation of multi-level encounter, von Hildebrand describes another mode of relatedness, formally distinct from encounter, which he calls "union" (*Vereinigung*). We have seen above his insistence that two persons can genuinely touch one another in a subject-to-subject relationship. But as he probes deeper into the intersubjective situation he discloses a new structure of relatedness, specifically distinct from encounter, in which two persons now not only contact one another as subjects, but join together in a unity that is possible only for personal beings. This constitutes a new phenomenon with a different formal essence, which, like the encounter situation, admits of a variety of modalities.

To begin with, it should be noted that the formal analysis of encounter-situations was neutral with respect to the establishment of some kind of union between the persons involved. Even the highest level of encounter, the simultaneous achievement of mutually revealed attitudes, could be concretely actualized as either togetherness in love or disparateness in hatred. For the material content of the attitudes expressed would be controlling. In all the essential types of interpersonal union that we are about to consider, however, it must be presupposed that the material content of the relationship is a positive rather than a negative one. It will then be the variations in the specific positive material content that will allow for various modes of union. Whereas the distinctions made of the phenomenon of encounter were based on the strictly formal structure of the different situations, von Hildebrand distinguishes specific kinds of unity-bonds in terms of the material meanings intended by the two persons. (How this affects the positive I-Thou love relationship we shall see later).

As encounter situations were formally of the I-Thou type, unity-situations are of the "we" type. Instead of being intentionally face-to-face, the two persons are, so to speak, side-by-side. Together they mutually expresses a common attitude or accomplish a common task. The formal structure of their relationship is not of the one-to-one type, but rather of the one-with-one kind.

Von Hildebrand describes various modalities of the we-situation, taking as a concrete example the common experience of a great danger, in which the consciousness of another's being present would essentially change the situation from that in which one underwent a similar experience alone.

First, there is a purely intentional contact. The other is 'there for me,' his presence colors my experience, modifies it, is a consolation for me in these circumstances, even if he is not conscious of my presence. Although he is in this case in no way an 'object' of my attitude or my attention, and although he may not even enter into my field of vision, he is still there for me – he stands near me in my lived experience.

A new level of contact is present when each of the two persons is aware of the other, when there is a mutual sharing of the other's consciousness of being nearby. Each is conscious that the other is aware of him; they feel together in the situation. Here a specific kind of contact – of 'nearby-ness' – first becomes real and breaks through the interpersonal space.[28]

For von Hildebrand, the distinctive mark of this kind of situation lies in this: Neither person expressly directs himself to the other as such; nor on the other hand does either one address the other. They do not so much face one another as stand by one another. Thus they structure a we-situation, quite different from an I-Thou encounter. The we-situation finds its fullest exemplification, finally, when persons join in a common enterprise in which each makes a necessary and distinctive contribution to the total effect. For in this case the product of their joint effort is clearly possible only if we have a we-subject. And those participating experience themselves *as* co-subjects; the structure of their relationship to one another is thus specifically different from an I-Thou situation. For in a we-situation each is expressly intending not a "face-to-face" encounter with the other, but a "lateral" bonding of a distinctive type. We might think, for example, of two musicians performing a musical piece. In such a case the individual experience of each player is clearly now not the same as if he were performing alone. For here he is not a performer but a co-performer. And each one consciously experiences himself as a participant in a we-situation.

It is interesting to compare von Hildebrand's descriptive analysis of the we-situation with the interpretation that Sartre gives of it. As we mentioned earlier, Sartre not only denies absolutely the possibility of an I-Thou en-

[28] "Zunächst eine rein intentionäre Berührung. Der andere ist 'für mich da,' seine Anwesenheit färbt mein Erleben, modifiziert es, bedeutet unter Umständen einen Trost für mich, auch wenn er von *meiner* Anwesenheit nichts weiss. Obgleich er in keiner Weise 'Objekt' meiner Stellungnahmen oder meines Kenntnisnehmens ist, obgleich er nicht in meinem Blickfeld steht, ist er doch für mich da – steht für mein Erlebnis neben mir.

Eine neue Stufe liegt vor, wenn *jede* der beiden Personen von der anderen weiss, wenn bei ihnen ein gegenseitig ineinandergreifendes Bewusstsein von dem 'Dabeisein' des – beziehungsgemäss – 'anderen' vorliegt und damit eine reale Berührung hergestellt ist. Jeder weiss, dass der andere von ihm weiss, man fühlt sich zusammen in dieser Situation. Hier wird diese eigenartige Berührung des 'Nebeneinander' erst *real*, greift durch den interpersonalen Raum hindurch." *MG.*, p. 35.

counter in which one could truly meet the other as subject, but he even insists that we-situations, too, come to be without any genuine subject-to-subject relationship arising between the participants. We-subjects arise for Sartre only in the face of a common enemy, an individual or a class. One wonders if he would find that the members of a symphony orchestra unite to play only because of the presence of an audience-enemy! It does seem that von Hildebrand's analysis – unhampered by a dialectical postulate – rings more true to one's ordinary experience.

There are three final points that should be made with respect to both of the basic structures of intersubjectivity, the I-Thou encounter and the we-situation, that we have been discussing in this chapter.

1. Following the practice of eidetic phenomenologists, von Hildebrand has been attempting to describe fundamental essential types of intersubjective situations. There are, he points out, less clearly defined situations which he would class reductively under one or other of the two basic types. For example, the social act creates a situation that does not fully exemplify either the I-Thou structure or the we-structure. For in the social act there is not the co-execution of acts typical of a "we" union. Nor does the social act intend an encounter with the being of the other, as does the I-Thou situation. But since all social acts direct an objective content to the other, von Hildebrand would class the social act reductively under the I-Thou type, noting, however, that it does not exhibit the full dimensions of this ideal type.

2. Since the two described types of intersubjective structuring are a priori possibilities von Hildebrand feels that we can utilize them in the analysis of every kind of relationship between persons singly or in groups. For in all association of persons the basic intentional posture will be either "facing-toward" the other person or standing "side-by-side."

3. Despite the distinction of these two essential types of relationship between persons von Hildebrand points out that they do not mutually exclude one another completely in an actual situation. Rather we usually find that though one intersubjective structure dominates the situation, individual acts within the total situation thus created may well be of the other type. For example, in the I-Thou situation structured by love, there will obviously be many times when the two persons function as a "we" in the co-execution of acts and attitudes. On the other hand, most forms of we-community will include many actual I-Thou encounters. As we shall see, the ground for the possibility of the most perfect co-execution of acts will thus be seen to be established by that highest form of I-Thou situation, mutually revealed love. For here, where persons are already closely united in love they can function

most perfectly as co-subjects of acts and attitudes toward others. Thus, despite the coexistence of both types of relationships within one and the same situation, there is always a clear distinction between them.

It may be useful to summarize briefly the main points of von Hildebrand's analysis that have been discussed in this chapter. Beginning with a consideration of the fundamental ambivalence of man as simultaneously the most self-contained being we know and as the being yet capable of the most intimate union with other persons, he outlines two basic forms which man's intersubjective existence may take, the I-Thou encounter and the we-union. The types of encounter and union that the person can establish he describes as totally different from those possible for nonpersonal being. For man can not only establish mere physical contact with another, but can establish a unique kind of relationship with other persons that may be either of an I-Thou or a "we" type. Each type admits of different degrees of realization. But beyond these two stages of interpersonal structuring, von Hildebrand describes another mode of relationship which we shall examine in the following chapter.

CHAPTER VII

THE EIDOS OF LOVE

The identification and description of the "I-Thou" and of the "we" situations according to their different eidetic structures constitutes only the first two stages in von Hildebrand's analysis of the basic types of intersubjective relationships. In addition to these, there is a third interpersonal situation that he selects for phenomenological scrutiny. This is the phenomenon of mutual love between persons.

Through a detailed analysis von Hildebrand attempts to identify the general essence of love and its various modalities. In love he sees exemplified to the highest degree that unique possibility which persons possess for entering into intersubjective relationships. For in love, he finds, persons go beyond "encounter" and beyond the kind of union achieved in a "we" situation to establish an essentially different kind of objective relationship, one which most properly fulfills man's potentiality for community with others.

It will be recalled that von Hildebrand begins his analysis of intersubjectivity by describing the human person as a paradox – he is the most self-contained being we know and at the same time the one most open to union with others. With the identification and description of the phenomenon of love, von Hildebrand feels that we reach the full dimensions of this paradox. For, in love, persons both retain their ontological identity and yet enter into the most encompassing kind of community. In his investigation of the underlying essence of the love relationship he therefore attempts to describe the different intentional acts that structure the love-situation and to determine the various modalities that present themselves in different kinds of love.

The groundwork for the analysis of this third basic mode of intersubjectivity has already been prepared in what we have seen thus far in the analysis of the stages of I-Thou encounter. The four levels there identified – from the unilateral intentional through the mutually revealed – were described according to their purely formal structure. It was pointed out that these formal structures could be fulfilled by a material content that was either positive or negative. Thus, for example, there could be mutually revealed negative attitudes reaching from mere disinterest or annoyance all the way to full expressed hatred. Similarly, there could be mutually revealed positive attitudes ranging from interest or esteem up to genuine love.

Now according to von Hildebrand's phenomenological classification, when we have a situation in which there is present both the fullest formal structure (mutually revealed attitudes) together with the highest material content (real hatred or genuine love), we have reached the fulfillment of interpersonal encounter. For in this instance, each person intends to focus and direct not merely his expression but his very being toward the being of the other. So, depending on whether it is love or hatred that structures the situation the consequences are these:

If it is mutual hatred that strikes through the interpersonal space between the two persons then they create a unique intersubjective situation marked by the greatest interpersonal distance and alienation. Though they may physically stand facing one another, they are intentionally at the ends of the earth from one another.

If, on the contrary, the expressed attitude is a positive rather than a negative one, then there is the possibility for a new kind of intersubjective situation to occur, one that is essentially different from "encounter."

For, when the mutually revealed attitude is one of genuine love – and not merely something akin to love such as esteem or gratitude – a completely new eidetic dimension is created in the interpersonal situation. When the material content is expressed mutual love, the essential structure of the situation can now no longer be described simply as an encounter. We have in this instance, says von Hildebrand, a radically different essential type. Expressed mutual love is not simply an encounter in which the material content is positive rather than negative. Rather love is a distinctive kind of situation different from and beyond "encounter," a situation whose eidetic description essentially includes the intending of some specific kind of union between the persons involved.

This unity-structure of a love-situation is seen as of a different kind from that union found in the "we" situation that was discussed in the previous chapter. For there the persons were joined as co-performers in a common enterprise. The dominant theme of their union was the common goal to be achieved or the common experiences undergone. The persons together faced a common task. In love, however, there is not a third factor to which they are directed. Rather, the dominant theme of the situation is precisely the other person in his being.

For von Hildebrand, the union of love thus comes not as the highest achievement of a we-relationship, but as the highest achievement of an I-Thou encounter-situation. In his view, situations structured by love exhibit a different essence from all other positive modes of interpersonal relationship principally by the fact that love creates an objective bond of union between the persons involved. Depending on the kind of love, the level of union intended may range from the bond of simple friendship up to the highest form of union found in spousal relationships. The I-Thou situation structured by love is thus more than an encounter. For the essence of all love means that persons not merely meet one another but become united, to some degree, in their very being. And this feature of union marks it off completely from all other positive modes of encounter where the revealed attitude though positive, is less than love.

The Eidetic Structure of Love

In his analysis of the eidos of love, von Hildebrand first examines the general structure of the love relationship and its various modalities. He comes then finally to a discussion of the highest mode of love relationship in which there is a genuine "becoming one" (*Einswerdung*) between persons. Our presentation of his views will follow the order of his analysis.

Love is a classical theme that has been discussed by philosophers from Plato to Sartre. Von Hildebrand's concept of love is essentially an altruistic one, and thus totally opposed to the self-aggrandizement theory of Sartre's that we have previously examined. The logical result of a whole-hearted attempt to found a philosophy of intersubjectivity on such a self-aggrandizement view of love we have seen in discussing the theory of Sartre. In the end such a view seems not only untrue to common experience, but also to be self-refuting. Where Sartre describes the subject as a gap in being attempting to overcome his nothingness by subduing the subjectivity of the other, von Hildebrand takes exactly the opposite view. For him, love is essentially a positive response to the objective and intrinsic value of the other's being. His concept of love is thus intimately related to his ethical theory.

We have mentioned earlier that von Hildebrand's phenomenological work has been largely devoted to moral and ethical studies, beginning with those which he published in Husserl's phenomenological *Jahrbuch* in its early years. His ethics is basically a value ethics similar to Scheler's. He holds that the person is a value-perceiving being as well as a merely cognitive one. Values are taken as objective dimensions of the state of affairs in which the person exists.

For von Hildebrand, therefore, "Love belongs to those attitudes of the person that are essentially responses to values. Just as reverence, wonder, respect, it can only be grounded on the value-character of the object to which it pertains."[1] Love is thus found to be present only when the other person is presented as in himself a being of intrinsic worth. Love is always a value-response, an attitude and act motivated by the genuine value of the other.

It is here that von Hildebrand finds realized fully that unique possibility of man for fulfillment through transcendance, through interesting himself in another precisely because of the intrinsic worth of the other. Such transcending love excludes all intention of self-aggrandizement. The basic ambivalance of the person which von Hildebrand points to in beginning his analysis of intersubjectivity is now seen in a fuller light. For in love the person both retains his self-identity and at the same time completely transcends all self-seeking in directing himself to the total personal being of the other.

Von Hildebrand feels that the many conflicting views of love that we find in the history of philosophy may be traced to a misunderstanding of this power of the human person for transcendence. He points out, for example, that even Plato is ambiguous and uncertain in his analysis of the meaning of love. Thus at times he describes it in terms that would make love a value response. At other times, as in the *Symposium,* the view is expressed by some of the speakers that love is the child of need and plenty. This concept of love could thus easily lead to the notion that in love the person seeks his own completion by assimilation of the beloved. Plato's indecision with regard to the essence of love was continued, according to von Hildebrand by Aristotle; here, however, the biological tendencies of Aristotle come more to the fore and the end-means relationship tends to overshadow the idea of love as an affective response to a genuine value.

A more faithful adherence to his own insight, von Hildebrand feels, would have shown Plato that the primary note in love is not the attempt to fill a need in the person; rather, love is characterized primarily by a self-donation of one person to the other. Love, he insists, cannot mean that we intend to use the other person as a *means* to our own happiness, and that we therefore attempt to assimilate the other. It represents, rather, the giving of an appropriate response to the perceived objective value of the other's personal being.

[1] "Die Liebe gehört zu den Stellungnahmen der Person, die wesenhaft auf einen Wert antworten. Wie Verehrung, Bewunderung, Begeisterung, Achtung kann sie nur durch einen Wertcharakter an dem Objekt, dem sie gilt, begründet werden." *MG.,* p. 40.

In his phenomenological studies of ethics von Hildebrand has explored the notion of the "adequate" value response in some detail, and Speigelberg assesses it as one of his "most original and influential conceptions."[2] In essence it means that the "ought" of an objective value demands not any response but one appropriate to the specific value in question. Once again, von Hildebrand seems to have sharpened and clarified an experience that is easily recognized as familiar. For we have all on occasion felt the disharmony of a situation in which we witness someone engrossed in worthless trivia and responding as if there were serious values involved. Conversely, we know how jarring an experience it can be to see someone respond inappropriately to a great work of art, to a Greek tragedy, for example, as if it were nothing but ancient "soap opera." In such a case the value response is totally inappropriate and inadequate.

If we now apply the notion of the adequate value response to the intersubjective situation, then von Hildebrand's phenomenological statement of the situation is this: When it is a person as such to whom an adequate value response is to be given, then the objective value of personal being dictates that the only adequate response from another person is some form of love. This does not mean that there may not be other appropriate responses to certain characteristics of the person; rather it means that when the very being of the other as such is that to which one directs oneself, then a love-response of some type is the appropriate one. How different situations are structured by different kinds of love-responses and when they are appropriate we shall see later.

Here, von Hildebrand feels, the great gap separating man from animal becomes strikingly clear. The animal is ruled by a strict teleology directed to his own self preservation and that of the species. Man is capable of much more than merely seeking his own completion, his intrinsic entelechy. Because he possessess the power of intending transcendence, he can direct himself to another being for the intrinsic, objective value which that being possesses. This ability of breaking through the closed circle of immanent self-aggrandizement to reach out to another person in an affective response to his true value, von Hildebrand counts as one of the most characteristic features of the human being. It manifests itself in all the affective responses, but especially does it reach its perfect form in mutual love.

Furthermore, he declares, the self-donation that is implied in all kinds of love does not mean a lessening of one's own being; rather, it shows the only way in which a person can truly fulfill his being. He sees the very essence of

[2] Spiegelberg, *op. cit.*, Vol. I, p. 222.

the human being as self-transcendence; and one who refuses to transcend himself by responding to objective values would thus cut himself off from the plenitude of the world of being and lock himself up in his own empty self. For, only by giving himself in full response to the world of values does man achieve his own happiness. Aristotle noted long ago that one cannot achieve happiness simply by willing it. For von Hildebrand, too, happiness comes always in the nature of a return, a gift, or a surplus. Only when one responds in appropriate fashion to a genuine value does happiness result.

These two principles, therefore, which von Hildebrand calls the principle of transcendence and the principle of superabundance, guide his analysis of love situations. "Love implies interest in another person for his own sake," he declares. "It must be rooted in the consciousness of the 'lovability' of the other person, the genuine abandonment to him, the consciousness that he deserves love. Only when love has this character of an authentic value response will true happiness flow into the lover's soul as a superabundant gift."[3]

Since von Hildebrand as an eidetic phenomenologist is concerned with the identification of the formal structure of intentional acts and attitudes, one might rightly expect to find that he subjects the phenomenon of love to detailed analysis. And such is indeed the case. He not only identifies basic constitutive elements at the core of the love-phenomenon, but in addition he distinguishes various essentially different types of love. Furthermore, in an effort to probe to the ontological value-conditions for a love relationship von Hildebrand attempts to show that love, being a value-response, comes about through what he calls the mutual "incorporation" of persons in a shared sphere of values. At this point therefore, we shall outline the main points he makes with respect to the essence of the love phenomenon, the varieties of love, and the relationship of love to values.

In general, as we have mentioned already, von Hildebrand identifies love as a response to the value of the personal being of another. It is thus an act of transcending, an "intending" of the other in a certain specific way. For a phenomenologist there can be identified various modes of "intending." We have discussed in connection with Scheler's theory of value-perception the notion of the emotional act as a special kind of "perception" – value perception – different from pure "cognitive" acts in the usual sense.

Von Hildebrand's value theory is similar to Scheler's in many ways. He, too, would hold that the affective dimension of man's being allows him to "perceive" values in the objective order, just as his cognitive dimension

[3] von Hildebrand, "Humanity at the Crossroads," *Thought*, XXIII (1948), 447–462, p. 454.

allows him to perceive other aspects of reality. But in his analysis of the value-response of love he goes much beyond Scheler.

The most essential feature he finds in the phenomenon of love as a value-response is that it always exhibits a *twofold* intending of the other person. The dual dimensions of this intending he identifies as the "intending of good" (intentio benevolentiae) and the "intending of union" (intentio unionis). The first is taken in the root sense of the Latin term *bene-volens,* as a "willing that the other enjoy good fortune." The second intention is a willing to be united with the other in some fashion. For von Hildebrand these constitute the invariant *formal* structure of the value-response of love. The variations in love situations arise from the different ways in which these formal intentions may be materially fulfilled.

Consistent with these variations, however, love always means an "intending of good" for the other. With the clarity of vision that love brings it perceives those things that constitute goods for the other and it attempts to secure them for him. Thus it shows itself in sacrifices for the other and in the loving care that one has for him. As for the intending of union with the other, von Hildebrand notes that all classical theories of love have pointed this out. But he feels that the meaning of union has not always been seen correctly, and he notes in particular the theories of Plato. As we have already remarked, the view expressed in Plato's *Symposium* does picture love as a union, but sees this union stemming from the unfulfilled "need" or lack that the person exhibits. Plato does not seem to see that intending union with the other is engendered by the perceived value of the person loved. This leads him to neglect the phenomenon of mutual love, the essence of which is not the absorption of the beloved, but that unique interpenetration of personal being by which at the highest level there is effected a "becoming-one" (*Einswerdung*).

Von Hildebrand's description of the stages of love relies on his earlier distinction of the four-fold level of I-Thou relationships. It will be recalled that at the first level the formal structure of an I-thou situation was purely intentional and not real, for it consisted only in an unrevealed attitude which one person directed toward another. Only with the next level, that of the revealed attitude, do we have a real reaching out to the other. When the attitude in question is not only a positive one (such as esteem or respect) but genuinely love, then the intersubjective situation can progress from a merely intentional one to the full reality of expressed mutual love in which each person intends union with the other. The unitive intention becomes real rather than merely intentional as soon as we have the transition from the non-revealed to the revealed attitude on the part of one person. "One's self-donation to the other becomes real through the fact that the inner 'word' of love becomes 'audible,' is perceived and received by the other, and thus actually reaches him as a person. In revealed love is found the climax of the communication of oneself to the other, the most unique and complete gift of oneself to him. Only in love does one give oneself thus."[4]

If the situation remains one-sided, however, and the other does not reciprocate, one cannot completely reach through to him. Only if he gives himself in his uniqueness, if he does not merely respond in a limited fashion, but actualizes his person in a completely reciprocal act of love does he fully reveal the entirety of his personal being and permit me to reach it. "As long as he remains only the object of my love, the one to whom it is addressed, I cannot reach him *as a person*," says von Hildebrand. "He is only fully involved as a person if he responds with love. As long as the beloved person does not reciprocally give himself to me in this unique way my love cannot grasp him. As long as he does not return the gaze of love I can never really reach the core of the other as a person."[5]

In the absence of mutual love, von Hildebrand allows of course that one can know and understand (*erkennen und verstehen*) the other person. But to truly encompass another person and remain united with him is possible only if he permits it by revealing himself fully and giving himself in the response of love. This mutual opening-up and expressed self-donation constitutes for von Hildebrand the formal structure within which there can be achieved that deepest mode of human union, a "becoming-one" in which each person in a unique way shares in the being of the other without violating the radical ontological independence of either.

Having identified the essence of the value-response of love as the twofold intending, the "unitive" and the "benevolent," von Hildebrand continues his eidetic analysis by distinguishing out a number of different forms of love.[6] The distinctions between them are made principally by reason of the different level which the unitive intention intends in any particular case.

[4] "Das sich zum ander *Hinbegeben* wird *real* dadurch, dass das innere 'Wort' der Liebe 'laut' wird, von der geliebten Person vernommen und aufgenommen wird, sie also als Person wirklich erreicht. In der verlautbarten Liebe liegt der Höhepunkt des sich Mitteilens an den andern, die eigentlichste und wirklichste *Hingabe* an ihn. Nur in der Liebe schenkt man sich selbst." *MG.*, p. 41.

[5] "Solange er nur Objekt und Adressat meiner Liebe ist, gelange ich nicht letztlich zu ihm als *Person*. Er ist als Person erst ganz hineinbezogen, wenn er die Liebe erwidert. Solange die geliebte Person nicht in dieser einzigartigen Weise sich zu mir *herbewegt,* entgleitet sie immer dem Griff meiner Liebe. Solange sie nicht den Blick der Liebe erwidert, kann ich sie als Person nie real an der zentralen Stelle erreichen." *MG.*, p. 42.

[6] In *MG.*, "Die 'Kategorien der Liebe,'" pp. 44–73.

For, though the twofold intending constitutes the formal structure of any love relationship, the kind of love that occurs will be determined by the material content of the intention. The case of "becoming-one" (*Einswerdung*) that we have mentioned is an instance in which the formal intending is specified in the highest possible way by a unitive relationship that seeks a true sharing of being through the total gift of oneself. Thus, not every form of love intends an *Einswerdung,* but every love must intend some mode of union with the other person. "In every genuine love there is essentially contained a unitive intention,"[7] von Hildebrand asserts. This, of course, might range all the way from the slight degree of union intended between neighbors through the closer kind proper to friendship, and up through progressively more intimate family relationships to the highest level of spousal *Einswerdung.*

Considering the broad range of various human relationships that fall within the general category of love in some sense, Von Hildebrand distinguishes certain basic types, "classical categories" of love, that condition the material distinctiveness of love. The categories he lists are broad ones; within each there could be, as he points out, further stratification without in any way crossing over into adjoining ones. All the types listed involve human love; he expressly omits any discussion of love toward God, understood in any sense. The distinction of certain categories of love is not original with von Hildebrand as he himself admits, though one must say that his attempt at a careful descriptive analysis of the precise essence of each type is unique.

These classical categories of love that he distinguishes are nine in number: 1) love of parents for children; 2) love of children for parents; 3) love of brothers and sisters for one another; 4) love for one simply as worthy of the love of a perceptive person; 5) love of friendship; 6) conjugal love; 7) holy love; 8) love of neighbor; 9) intellectual love.

Since our purpose is only to outline the main lines of von Hildebrand's phenomenology of intersubjectivity we do not intend to discuss here each of these types of love. Rather we shall mention only two for purposes of illustration. It should be noted, however, that in the actual descriptive analysis of all these types emphasis is placed on the definitive role played by variations in the material content of the specific unitive and "benevolent" intending. While all love-situations will manifest this twofold intending as constituting the situation-structure, there can be great variety in the actual content of the intending – in what kind of union is intended and what kinds of goods are willed for the other.

[7] "In jeder echten Liebe ist wesentlich eine intentio unitiva enthalten." *MG.,* p. 44.

It should be noted, further, that within the nine general categories certain affiliations appear. Thus conjugal love and holy love are found to resemble one another. In both there is an exclusive dominance of the I-Thou structure and in both the intending of the highest mode of love. Similarly, sibling love and love of friendship are seen to exhibit much the same form; in both there is less of a "facing toward" each other, and more resemblance to the "we" union. Such similarities, however, are not found to be so great as to lessen the independence of these categories from one another. Thus, speaking as the eidetic phenomenologist engaged in the search for distinguishable essences von Hildebrand remarks: "Mother love may be ever so great, ever so deep and directed toward the welfare of the children; it still remains mother love and as such is categorically distinct from the love of friendship or conjugal love."[8]

In a full phenomenological categorization, he points out, attention would have to be paid to the general differences which love in each category manifests insofar as it concerns two persons of the same or of opposite sex. "Masculinity and femininity are not only biological characteristics, but they signify a profound distinctiveness in the structure of the spiritual person."[9] With the inclusion of this factor a new dimension appears in each category. If we are dealing with conjugal love, sexual distinctiveness is of course the very foundation for the identity of the category, and not merely an additional dimension. But within other types, such as friendship love or sibling love, it is an important, but added factor to the already constituted category.

Although we do not intend to present here the detailed analyses of the various types of love enumerated above, brief mention will be made of two of them – parental love and conjugual love. The first of these will illustrate a category in which the unitive intention does not aim at *Einswerdung*. The identification of conjugal love will prepare for a consideration of the presuppositions that von Hildebrand sees required in order that *Einswerdung* can take place.

Parental love: Here, as in the case of the other categories, von Hildebrand provides a lengthy descriptive analysis in order to bring out the specific essence of the intersubjective structure in question. The following selected

[8] "Die Mutterliebe mag noch so gross sein, sie mag noch so tief sein und auf das Heil des Kindes abzielen: sie bleibt immer Mutterliebe und als solche kategorial verschieden von der Freundesliebe oder der ehelichen Liebe." *MG.*, p. 47.

[9] "'Weiblich' und 'mannlich' sind nicht nur *biologische Charaktere,* sondern bedeuten auch tiefgehende Formverschiedenheiten der *geistigen Person* des Menschen." *MG.*, p. 47.

excerpts from his description may serve to illustrate the main points by which this category is distinguished:

> [Prescinding now from the distinction between father-love and mother-love, parental love in general] is a distinct type in which there is not found a specific 'standing vis-a-vis each other' as in conjugal love. Here the mutuality of love is not so constituent a factor of meaningfulness as in conjugal love . . . [If we may characterize the brother-sister love and also the love of friendship, as a 'standing beside one another,'] then here, to continue the spatial metaphor, the parental love is rather a 'standing behind the child.' The parents stand behind the child, as it were, protecting him and embracing him. Their love does not contain specifically an inner appeal to the child to remain faced toward them. Rather, parental love expressly intends that the child should face out toward the world, to life and its tasks. This is the most characteristic mark of parental love, this loving 'over the head of the child.'. . . In parental love we find also that the 'willing of good' *(intentio benevolentiae)* is more determining than the 'willing of union' *(intentio unionis)*. Each intention here of course is of a special kind [compared with that intended in conjugal love.] . . . Parental love does not aim at an *Einswerdung,* but rather at an actual 'remaining beside' the loved person . . . The mutual love here is thus of a different kind: it requires a return of love from the child that is of a specifically different type, and not [as we see in conjugal love] a return of the same kind of love. . . . . The 'willing of good' (*intentio benevolentiae*) has here this special characteristic that it urges the child more and more to independence, to 'stand on his own feet,' to develop himself as a unique person. The child is to be educated for the road of life and the loving care of the parents makes him ever more capable of setting out on that road. In parental love, therefore, the two fundamental intentions of love are necessarily in conflict, so to speak, and thus there is a certain tragic note in all earthly parental love.[10]

[10] ". . . Sie ist eine Liebe, in der nicht ein spezifisches Sich-gegenüber-Stehen vorliegt – wie in der ehelichen Liebe. Dies kommt schon darin zum Ausdruck, dass hier die Liebe ihrem Sinn nach nicht derart auf Gegenliebe abzielt, wie es die eheliche Liebe tut. . . . Es ist vielmehr, um bei diesem räumlichen Bild zu bleiben, ein 'Hintereinanderstehen.' Die Eltern stehen 'hinter' dem Kind – es beschirmend und von oben her umfassend. Ihre spezifische Liebe enthält als solche nicht den inneren Appell an das Kind, sich den Eltern mit dem Antlitz zuzuwenden. Vielmehr umfasst diese Liebe in einer Weise, bei der das Antlitz des Kindes ausdrücklich dem Leben, seinen Aufgaben und Arbeiten, zugewandt wird. Es ist ein spezifisches Lieben der anderen Person über ihren Kopf hinweg. . . . in ihr die intentio benevolentiae vor der intentio unitiva einen Vorsprung hat. Doch ist bei ihr sowohl die intentio unitiva wie die intentio benevolentiae von ganz eigener Art. . . . Sie zielt nicht auf eine *Einswerdung* im Ineinanderblick ab, wohl aber auf ein wirkliches 'Weilen' bei der geliebten Person, . . . Gegenliebe wird also ersehnt, wenn auch nicht eine völlige, gleichartige Zuwendung; . . . Die intentio benevolentiae in ihrer besonderen Ausprägung drängt hier sogar dazu, das Kind immer mehr auf 'seine eigenen Füsse zu stellen' und die eigene Person überflüssig zu machen. Das Kind wird für den Weg in 'Leben' erzogen, und die liebende Sorgfalt der Eltern macht es gleichsam immer fähiger zum 'Auszug' ins Leben. In diesem Widerstreit der beiden der Liebe grundwesentlichen Intentionen liegt eine gewisse Tragik der Elternliebe auf Erden. *MG.,* p. 48–50.

Conjugal love: This of course occupies a unique position in any discussion of love.[11] For von Hildebrand it is essentially marked by the dominance of the unitive intention, though the "benevolent" intention is not lacking, since its characteristic feature is the intending of the total gift of self to the other. Therefore the mutuality of love is here essential; both persons desire and intend it. There results thus a comprehension of the total value of the other, an awareness of his specific person-value. Through this, the other becomes, as it were, transparent; his full value as this specific person, unique and unlike any other is revealed. Because of this total character of conjugal love, there is the possibility for achieving within it, a genuine "becoming one" with the other. This, however, can only take place when certain conditions are fulfilled with respect to the value-situation within which the relationship occurs. Before discussing the conditions required for two persons to achieve a "becoming one" (*Einswerdung*), von Hildebrand therefore sets forth a more detailed explanation of how values function in the coming into being of a love relationship.

Value as Bonding Medium

Von Hildebrand's value-theory is an emphatically realistic one. Values for him are actual dimensions of reality and not merely subjectively imposed categories. The fact that they are not perceptible in the same sense as physical qualities, he admits. But for that matter, he points out, much of our experience relates to non-sensible dimensions of reality. Unless one is prepared to hold a simplistic, nineteenth-century type of materialism, one's notion of what is real must make room for much that is not perceptible matter. As we mentioned earlier, von Hildebrand vigorously defends the application of the terms "objective" and "real" to acts and attitudes of the human subject as against any psychological reductionism that would dismiss such phenomena as "merely psychological" states. He extends this same designation of "real and objective" to intersubjective situations as well as to the acts by which these are generated. And he would say that such situations, involving one person vis-a-vis another, should be considered as far more real than any juxtaposition of merely physical beings.

Consistent with this view, therefore, von Hildebrand classifies genuine values as real and objective structures of man's world. Furthermore, he holds with Scheler that man is gifted with a unique value-perception which

[11] Von Hildebrand has treated this type of love in a separate book, *Marriage,* New York, Longmans, 1942.

functions in its own sphere – the affective dimension of man – much as cognitive perception functions in its own neutral, valueless sphere.

How then does this value theory enter into von Hildebrand's phenomenology of love? In a number of ways. There is first, as we have already mentioned, the fact that all positive emotional attitudes and acts are seen as responses to some value in the other person. When the act is one of love itself, this represents a specific response not to some isolated quality of the other, but *to the other's being as a person perceived in its value-dimension.*

Beyond this general description of love as a value response to the other, however, von Hildebrand's analysis goes much further. We have already pointed out that the unitive intention is present, in all genuine love, with various modalities depending on the specific formal structure of the situation, such as parental love, spousal love, etc. In his further analysis of the role of values von Hildebrand makes two additional points. First, the possibility of any fulfillment of the unique unitive intention that is essential to love comes about *because values provide an objective bonding medium through which persons are united.* Secondly, the material difference in the quality and depth of love within any formal category is attributable to the level of the values involved. We shall begin our consideration of the first point with a discussion of the various modes of the realization or "incorporation" of values.

As has been mentioned earlier, the ability of man to respond to values is regarded as a unique mark of his power of transcending himself. Beyond the capability of neutral cognition of the world about him, man is able to interest himself in goods for their own sake; unlike the animal he is not merely a conditioned self-perfecting entelechy whose actions are guided solely by the end of intrinsic development. This capability of value response is thus the prerogative of man alone. "Man is the only being who exhibits this kind of orientation toward values. His being is structured in such a way that he is able to penetrate through to values and to grasp them understandingly. He is able to respond to them, and his responses take many forms, such as joy, admiration, enthusiasm, esteem, reverence, love." [12]

Beyond the power of responding to values, man is seen, too, as having the power to create values, as in works of art, in intellectual achievements, or in moral acts. Some values present themselves with a certain universal

[12] Allein von dieser Hinordnung und Zuordnung aus ist das Wesen des Menschen zu verstehen. Der Mensch ist in seiner Struktur so aufgebaut, dass er diese Welt der Werte verstehend zu erfassen, dass er sie erkennend zu durchdringen vermag. Er ist fähig, sie zu beantworten in der mannigfachsten Weise, in Stellungnahmen der Freude, der Bewunderung, der Begeisterung, der Achtung, der Verehrung, der Liebe." *MG.*, p. 74.

"ought" attached, such as ethical or religious ones. But for the most part there is wide latitude with respect to the other various spheres of value that one is interested in or attracted to. Each person has a special distinctiveness and talent that makes it possible for him to live in certain worlds of value and not in others. Thus, a gifted artist lives in a world that is closed to someone who lacks similar talents and similar value perception. Another person may dwell in a world of intellectual, religious, or social values.

Now, for von Hildebrand, this giving of oneself to a specific world of values effects what he calls a double "incorporation" or actualization of the values in question. "On the one hand the value-sphere in question is realized in a certain sense, in the person – on the other hand, this value-sphere receives the person into itself." [13] There are several meanings which could be attached to the notion of a "realization" of values, and von Hildebrand distinguishes them. There is first of all, the realization that a value has in the being that is the "bearer" (*Träger*) of the value. If we talk of artistic values, for example, then it is the work of art itself that in a very special and proper sense is the actual bearer of the value; for it is in the work itself that the value first comes into being and perdures as long as the art-work exists.

Distinct from this primary actualization, however, von Hildebrand identifies a further realization that this artistic value has in the person by his value-response to the work of art. For the value-response is neither mere knowledge of the art-object, nor technical understanding about it, but rather a totally distinctive act of appreciation in which the value is given a new and unique kind of actualization. Of course, the value is not said to inhere in the person as it does in the art-object itself. "Rather it begins to dwell in him – it extends its sway out over his person." [14] It is therefore a new existence for the value, distinct from that which it has in the work of art. It is a realization that is made possible by the trancendent nature of man, open to the world of values and capable of value-response. This kind of realization of value admits of a further distinction. For, while every actual act of value-response to an art-work represents a particular actualization of the value in question in the one who appreciates it, one could speak of a more extensive realization in a person who is specifically oriented toward the world of art as a dominant value-sphere. In this case there would be the realization not of a single value but of the world of art-values.

[13] "Einerseits wird der betreffende Wertbereich in gewissem Sinn *in der betreffenden Person realisiert* – andrerseits *nimmt der Wertbereich die Person in sich auf.*" *MG.*, p. 75.

[14] "Sie 'nehmen' vielmehr nur in ihm 'Wohnung' – sie dehnen ihren Herrschaftsbereich über seine Person hin aus." *MG.*, p. 76.

This then, is the first phase of the dual realization that von Hildebrand describes. In it some particular value or value-sphere begins to exist in a new fashion through the acts and attitudes of the person who responds to it. The second phase of incorporation consists in a certain reciprocal "embodiment" of the person in the sphere of values he responds to. "The person is encompassed by this value-sphere – he is in a sense drawn into it and embodied in it."[15] Von Hildebrand believes that phenomenological analysis would reveal that each person becomes embodied in this way in numerous value-spheres. For he sees man existing as a being whose value-perception opens up to him a great range of value-spheres that exist objectively. Thus, no one can be totally blind to values, though wide variations in value-sensitivity exist.

But in addition to this general openess toward many sets of values, persons are oriented primarily toward one value-sphere which plays a dominant role in their life. "This it is *in* which a man lives and *out* of which he lives."[16] This dominant value-sphere is therefore not only that to which he most gives realization, but even more important, it is that which shapes his being and within which he exists. It becomes his "world," and from its perspective he views all else. Thus there are persons who live almost totally in the scientific world of values, or in that of the artistic. Obviously this second phase of the "dual incorporation" is much more important than the first. For here the being-structure of the person is affected by the determination it receives from the influence of his primary and dominant world of values. "His very being is deeply stamped by this sphere."[17]

Given the fact that we have this dual incorporation possible in the realm of values, how does this relate to von Hildebrand's phenomenology of love? To answer that question we must recall two basic points about his concept of love that were mentioned previously: First, love is identified as a value response not to an isolated quality in the other, but to him as a totality, to the specific value of the other's being now seen as domiciled in and structured by his dominant value-sphere. Secondly, love always intends some kind of union between the persons involved. This union is of a distinctive kind only possible for personal beings and finds no counterpart among beings of a lesser order.

Now for von Hildebrand it is the fact of value-incorporation that makes this unique union possible. In his view this union is achieved because each

[15] "Die Person wird von dem Wertbereich dabei umfangen – sie wird in diese Wertsphäre in einem gewissen Sinne 'einverleibt.'" *MG.*, p. 78.

[16] "... sie ist es, *in* der der Mensch lebt und *aus* der er lebt." *MG.*, p. 78.

[17] "... ihr Wesen ist von dieser Sphäre noch tiefer geprägt." *MG.*, p. 79.

person, through his response to the value of the being of the other, thereby effects a new and double realization of that person-value: It is incorporated in him and he is embodied in it. In the case of mutual love there is thus a joint exchange and sharing *in the other's being-as-value.* The existence of value as an objective dimension of the person, and the capability man has to transcend the limits of his own being through his response to values, thus explains how it is possible for the union intended in love to be achieved.

In this way von Hildebrand proposes to explain – but not to dissolve – the "paradox of subjectivity" that he pointed out at the start of his analysis of intersubjectivity. He there described the human subject as the being who exhibits both the most inviolable individuality and yet the greatest potentiality for fulfillment through union with other personal beings. Achieving such union without dissolving the boundaries of the individual beings involved is seen as possible only because of the unique power of the person to transcend the limits of his being and to respond to the person-value of another. For by this response he unites himself to the other with a double bond: He incorporates the other's being-as-value within himself and at the same time he himself becomes embodied in the other's value-being. In this way, persons are joined together in a unity that is real and objective, though not physical. The achievement of this kind of bonding is one of the most distinctive marks of personal beings, and it is this that constitutes the union intended in love.

That, in brief, is the general role von Hildebrand assigns to values in his analysis of any intersubjective situation that is structured by a love relationship. But there are several important distinctions that he adds.

To begin with, even though it is the value of the other person as such that calls forth a response, there are usually other specific values in the other that serve as a starting-point for the perception of the person-value of the other in its totality. Von Hildebrand mentions a number of different kinds of values that could serve as such a starting point. They could be life values, such as temperament or charm; intellectual values, such as wit, humor, intellectual versatility; they could be social values such as culture, courtesy, fine manners; ethical values, such as sincerity, fidelity, generosity.

Beyond the initial response to such specific values, however, each person in any kind of love relationship finds that he is led on to appreciate and respond to the person-value of the other as such. Since each person ordinarily has manifold relationships with others who embody different value-spheres – such as those of science, art, religion – he finds that these relationships open up wholly different worlds for him. Furthermore, since his response to these new value-spheres is made in a shared, and not an individual fashion, each becomes "embodied" in these value-spheres in a different way as a partner than he would as an individual.

At this point, as von Hildebrand admits, a difficulty appears. His analysis of a mutual-love situation would seem to require that both persons be domiciled in the same dominant value sphere. For it is by response to the other person in his concrete being-as-value that love achieves union. Must we say, therefore, that such a relationship is possible only between persons who are fundamentally incorporated in the same sphere of values, or is it also possible to have such an interpersonal union when two persons are situated in very different value spheres? Can we, for example, have a love relationship between, say, a deeply spiritual person and one essentially oriented toward the sphere of life-values?

Ideally, says von Hildebrand, each person should be incorporated in the same dominant value-sphere even in love of friendship. For when both come to the relationship with the same dominant value-sphere, this mutual embodiment in the identical sphere of values creates a bond of the closest kind between them. But in actual fact, we often find that persons in a relationship of mutual love – of friendship, for example – do not have the same dominant value-sphere. In this case, says von Hildebrand, there must be some other value-sphere which they respond to in common in order for a genuine love relationship to develop. For this less central sphere of values then serves as a common "place"[18] where these two persons coincide, as an aperture through which each can apprehend the total personal value of the other.

Thus it is clear that persons situated in different dominant value-spheres can nevertheless share a common third, and this sharing opens up the possibility for structuring that kind of union in their value-being that is required for any kind of love relationship to develop. This lack of coincidence of dominant value-spheres is often found in love of friendship or sibling love, and many times, too, even in conjugal love. But where there is this lack of coincidence, the relationship – even though it may be one of conjugal love – can never reach that utmost kind of unity possible between personal beings, the union that von Hildebrand calls "becoming one" (*Einswerdung*).

For the achievement of that highest degree of interpersonal union, von Hildebrand finds that certain definite conditions must be met.[19] To begin with, of course, the intersubjective relationship in question must be of the basic I-Thou type. And it must be one that is structured by love that is both expressed and mutual. Given a love-situation, *Einswerdung* then requires

[18] "eine bestimmte Stelle." *MG.*, p. 95.

[19] See *MG.*, pp. 104–110.

that each of the two intentions which constitute the invariant structure of love (the unitive and the "benevolent" intentions) be realized in the highest possible way.

Fulfilling the unitive intention to the utmost requires first, that both persons must live in the same dominant value sphere. For both must consciously intend the closest possible union and sharing in one another's being. And according to von Hildebrand's analysis of the dual incorporation effected by all values responses, two persons can become united in the closest possible way only when they effect a simultaneous and mutual dual incorporation of each other's value-being as it is embodied in an identical sphere of values.

Sharing the same dominant value-sphere is still only the *formal* condition required for making possible the highest fulfillment of the unitive intention of love. There is required also – as a *material* condition – that the common and shared value-sphere be that specific one in which the very essence of man as a personal being-of-value is encompassed. For only when the value-response of love reaches to that value-sphere that expresses the ultimate meaning of man as a personal being can the union effected be one that truly binds persons together in the totality of their being-as-persons. Only then is there achieved both a formal coincidence of personal beings (they share the same dominant value-sphere), and a material coincidence (the common sphere coincides with the one that is most essential to man's being as a person). With this double coincidence, the true value-being of each person is mutually embodied in the other. They have become one in a distinctive and unique way.

Concretely, then, which value-sphere is it that must be the common and dominant one if this material condition is to be fulfilled? For von Hildebrand – who takes man as essentially a being of spirit – the dominant value-sphere required for the achievement of *Einswerdung* must be the sphere of spiritual values. For he sees man's ability to live in and respond to spiritual values as the paramount power of personal being. He admits, of course, that mutual love – even conjugal love – can be grounded on lesser spheres of values. Love can be found even where persons do not share the same dominant value sphere, as was mentioned earlier. But for the realization of the highest possibility of mutual love, in which there is effected the closest of human unions, a true "becoming-one" (*Einswerdung*), he finds it necessary that both persons be domiciled in the sphere of spiritual values. For only by mutually responding to man's value as a being of spirit does one reach personal being in its essence.

When the above conditions are met, the unitive intention of love can be eminently fulfilled. But for the achievement of *Einswerdung,* the second basic intention – the willing of good – must reach its highest material fulfillment also. This means that each person must consciously will and attempt to gain for the other the greatest good that could be realized for him as a being of spirit and value. How one conceives this greatest good in the concrete, will depend, of course, on how one understands the meaning of spiritual fulfillment. History testifies to the wide variety of views on this point. Von Hildebrand, because of his own Judeo-Christian religious beliefs, finds this concept of the greatest personal good fulfilled in the traditional idea of salvation. But since his phenomenological analysis of the essence and kinds of intersubjective relationships is such a formal one, other and different concepts of personal spiritual fulfillment would fit in equally well.

In this ultimate realization of mutual love, this "becoming one" (*Einswerdung*) von Hildebrand thus finds an eidetic structure that is essentially different from all others. For only here does the unitive intention mean the greatest possible mutual sharing of personal being. And only here does the intention of willing good for the other mean materially the greatest possible good. In all love-situations other than that of *Einswerdung,* one or both of these two basic intentions stops short of total fulfillment in either a formal or a material way.

The significance of value-theory in von Hildebrand's phenomenology of intersubjectivity can thus be seen to be central. For he does not merely assert that love is to be regarded as a value-response, but he develops an extremely detailed analysis to show how this can be so. Through all the various categories of love which he enumerates, values provide the basis for the initiation of those acts and attitudes toward the other that establish the categorically distinct situations. Value-responses thus establish the bonds between persons. For with them we have the intending of the being of one person toward the person-value inherent in the other. The objective and real bonds between persons are thus value-bonds.

We can see the vast differences there are between this phenomenology of intersubjectivity and that of Sartre's. Cut off from all values except those that he makes for himself, the Sartrean man is caught in a whirlpool of self-interest. The "making of self" which he sets as his goal is from the beginning doomed to failure. Sartre allows for no transcendence that would permit a subject-to-subject encounter, much less any true personal union. Von Hildebrand's analysis of the subject and intersubjectivity sees man oriented in a totally opposite fashion. The last remnants of the isolated Cartesian subject are banished. Instead we have man conceived as an open-ended process of transcendence. He is open to a whole world of values stretching from those of physical nature to the totally different realm of personal values.

We can now see more clearly too why von Hildebrand begins his analysis of intersubjectivity with a discussion of the varying types of unity and individuality that are found among physical beings. The limits of physical beings are such that they can be conjoined with other physical beings only in purely external juxtaposition. Any mode of union beyond that would cause their individuality to be submerged in some greater totality. Using physical modes of individuality and union as a basis for comparison he wishes to illustrate the essentially different types of relationships that can be established between persons. For as intentional beings and beings of spirit they can enter into a mode of contact, the "encounter," that is impossible for physical beings. Furthermore, because persons can perceive and respond to values, they can enter into types of union in which objective relationships are mutually established that far surpass anything possible in the world of matter. Persons united in the highest mode of love can even "become one." And yet this "becoming-one" does not mean that the boundaries of each individual person are abolished. It does not mean, as Scheler held, that all emerge out of a common, all-encompassing stream of life and so shade off into one another in their psychic lives. Rather as beings of intentionality and of spirit persons retain their absolute self-contained individuality even while they transcend themselves to become one with another in mutual love.

INDEX